International Technical Support Organization

WebSphere for z/OS Connectivity Architectural Choices

December 2004

SG24-6365-00

Note: Before using this information and the product it supports, read the information in "Notices" on page vii.

First Edition (December 2004)

This edition applies to Version 5, Release 1 of WebSphere Application Server for z/OS.

© **Copyright International Business Machines Corporation 2004. All rights reserved.**
Note to U.S. Government Users Restricted Rights -- Use, duplication or disclosure restricted by GSA ADP Schedule Contract with IBM Corp.

Contents

Notices vii
Trademarks viii

Preface ix
The team that wrote this redbook. ix
Become a published author xii
Comments welcome. xii

Chapter 1. Architectural considerations 1
1.1 The connectivity conundrum 2
1.2 The first decision point 3
1.3 Asynchronous versus synchronous. 4
1.4 Asynchronous transactions: A developer's view 5
1.5 z/OS concepts and terminology 6
1.6 WebSphere concepts and terminology 7
1.7 Transaction management concepts and terminology 8
1.8 WebSphere for z/OS clustering. 9
1.9 WebSphere for z/OS failover and load-balancing 10
1.10 Types of WebSphere connections 11
1.11 Local connections 12
    1.11.1 Local connection: Attributes 13
1.12 Remote connections 14
    1.12.1 Remote connection: Attributes 15
1.13 Local connection with some availability. 16
1.14 Remote connection with availability 17

Chapter 2. DB2 connectivity options. 19
2.1 Accessing DB2 from a Java program 20
2.2 JDBC driver types 22
    2.2.1 Type 1. 23
    2.2.2 Type 2. 23
    2.2.3 Type 3. 23
    2.2.4 Type 4. 23
2.3 Connecting from WebSphere to DB2 on z/OS 24
2.4 Different connectivity scenarios. 26
2.5 Local DB2 connection 27
    2.5.1 Local DB2 connection: Attributes 28
2.6 Remote DB2 connection 30
    2.6.1 Remote DB2 connection: Attributes 31

© Copyright IBM Corp. 2004. All rights reserved.   **iii**

2.7 Mixed DB2 configuration: local T2 and remote T4 33
2.8 Mixed DB2 configuration: Local and remote with the same T4 driver . . . 35
2.9 Comparing DB2 performance 36
2.10 Local DB2 with availability. 37
2.11 Remote DB2 with availability. 39
2.12 Security options. 40
2.13 Security considerations for DB2 connections 42
2.14 Migration from legacy JDBC driver to T2 UD 43
2.15 SQLJ 45

Chapter 3. CICS connectivity options 49
3.1 CICS connection architectural choices 50
3.2 The resource adapter 51
3.3 CICS Transaction Gateway. 54
   3.3.1 EXCI pipes 55
3.4 Local CICS connection 56
   3.4.1 Local CICS connection: Attributes 57
3.5 Remote connection to CICS TG in same LPAR 61
   3.5.1 Remote connection to CICS TG in same LPAR: Attributes 62
3.6 Remote CICS connection 64
   3.6.1 Remote CICS connection: Attributes 65
3.7 Local CICS with increased availability. 68
   3.7.1 Local CICS with increased availability: Attributes 69
3.8 Routing CICS local to remote 72
   3.8.1 Routing CICS local to remote: Attributes 74
3.9 Remote CICS with availability 77
   3.9.1 Remote CICS with availability: Attributes 79
3.10 Remote with availability using CICS routing 81
   3.10.1 Remote availability with CICS routing: Attributes 82
3.11 Accessing CICS using RMI/IIOP. 85
   3.11.1 Accessing CICS using RMI over IIOP: Attributes 87
3.12 CICS RMI over IIOP with availability. 91
   3.12.1 CICS RMI/IIOP with availability: Attributes 92
3.13 SOAP connection 93
   3.13.1 SOAP connection: Attributes. 94

Chapter 4. IMS connectivity options 97
4.1 Interface components: Resource adapter 98
4.2 Interface components: IMS Connect. 100
4.3 Local IMS connection 102
   4.3.1 Local IMS connection: Attributes. 103
4.4 Local IMS connection in the same sysplex 106
   4.4.1 Local IMS connection in same sysplex: Attributes 107

4.5 Local IMS connection: High availability 110
    4.5.1 Local IMS connection with availability: Attributes 111
4.6 Remote IMS in same sysplex: Availability 113
    4.6.1 Remote connection with availability: Attributes 114
4.7 Remote IMS in different sysplexes 117
    4.7.1 Remote IMS in different sysplexes: Attributes 118
4.8 IMS security flow: Container-managed 120
4.9 IMS security flow: Component-managed 122
4.10 JDBC for IMS 123

Chapter 5. WebSphere MQ connectivity options 125
5.1 Local MQ connectivity: Bindings mode 126
    5.1.1 Binding mode: Attributes 127
5.2 Remote MQ connectivity: Client mode 129
    5.2.1 Client mode: Attributes 130
5.3 WebSphere MQ connectivity with availability 132
5.4 Increasing availability with shared queues 134
5.5 WebSphere MQ access to CICS and IMS 136
    5.5.1 WebSphere MQ-CICS bridge 136
    5.5.2 WebSphere MQ-IMS bridge 137

Appendix A. Additional material 139
Locating the Web material 139
Using the Web material 139
    How to use the Web material 140

Related publications 141
IBM Redbooks 141
Other publications 141
Online resources 142
How to get IBM Redbooks 142
Help from IBM 142

Abbreviations and acronyms 143

Index 145

Contents   **v**

vi   WebSphere for z/OS Connectivity Architectural Choices

Notices

This information was developed for products and services offered in the U.S.A.

IBM may not offer the products, services, or features discussed in this document in other countries. Consult your local IBM representative for information on the products and services currently available in your area. Any reference to an IBM product, program, or service is not intended to state or imply that only that IBM product, program, or service may be used. Any functionally equivalent product, program, or service that does not infringe any IBM intellectual property right may be used instead. However, it is the user's responsibility to evaluate and verify the operation of any non-IBM product, program, or service.

IBM may have patents or pending patent applications covering subject matter described in this document. The furnishing of this document does not give you any license to these patents. You can send license inquiries, in writing, to:
IBM Director of Licensing, IBM Corporation, North Castle Drive Armonk, NY 10504-1785 U.S.A.

The following paragraph does not apply to the United Kingdom or any other country where such provisions are inconsistent with local law: INTERNATIONAL BUSINESS MACHINES CORPORATION PROVIDES THIS PUBLICATION "AS IS" WITHOUT WARRANTY OF ANY KIND, EITHER EXPRESS OR IMPLIED, INCLUDING, BUT NOT LIMITED TO, THE IMPLIED WARRANTIES OF NON-INFRINGEMENT, MERCHANTABILITY OR FITNESS FOR A PARTICULAR PURPOSE. Some states do not allow disclaimer of express or implied warranties in certain transactions, therefore, this statement may not apply to you.

This information could include technical inaccuracies or typographical errors. Changes are periodically made to the information herein; these changes will be incorporated in new editions of the publication. IBM may make improvements and/or changes in the product(s) and/or the program(s) described in this publication at any time without notice.

Any references in this information to non-IBM Web sites are provided for convenience only and do not in any manner serve as an endorsement of those Web sites. The materials at those Web sites are not part of the materials for this IBM product and use of those Web sites is at your own risk.

IBM may use or distribute any of the information you supply in any way it believes appropriate without incurring any obligation to you.

Information concerning non-IBM products was obtained from the suppliers of those products, their published announcements or other publicly available sources. IBM has not tested those products and cannot confirm the accuracy of performance, compatibility or any other claims related to non-IBM products. Questions on the capabilities of non-IBM products should be addressed to the suppliers of those products.

This information contains examples of data and reports used in daily business operations. To illustrate them as completely as possible, the examples include the names of individuals, companies, brands, and products. All of these names are fictitious and any similarity to the names and addresses used by an actual business enterprise is entirely coincidental.

COPYRIGHT LICENSE:
This information contains sample application programs in source language, which illustrates programming techniques on various operating platforms. You may copy, modify, and distribute these sample programs in any form without payment to IBM, for the purposes of developing, using, marketing or distributing application programs conforming to the application programming interface for the operating platform for which the sample programs are written. These examples have not been thoroughly tested under all conditions. IBM, therefore, cannot guarantee or imply reliability, serviceability, or function of these programs. You may copy, modify, and distribute these sample programs in any form without payment to IBM for the purposes of developing, using, marketing, or distributing application programs conforming to IBM's application programming interfaces.

© Copyright IBM Corp. 2004. All rights reserved.   **vii**

Trademarks

The following terms are trademarks of the International Business Machines Corporation in the United States, other countries, or both:

AIX®	Eserver®	RACF®
CICS®	eServer™	Redbooks (logo) ™
CICSPlex®	FICON®	Redbooks (logo)™
DB2 Universal Database™	ibm.com®	Redbooks™
DB2®	IBM®	S/390®
Distributed Relational Database	IMS™	TXSeries®
Architecture™	Informix®	WebSphere®
DRDA®	MQSeries®	z/OS®
e-business on demand™	MVS™	zSeries®
@server®	OS/390®	
@server®	Parallel Sysplex®	

The following terms are trademarks of other companies:

Microsoft, Windows, and the Windows logo are trademarks of Microsoft Corporation in the United States, other countries, or both.

Java and all Java-based trademarks and logos are trademarks or registered trademarks of Sun Microsystems, Inc. in the United States, other countries, or both.

UNIX is a registered trademark of The Open Group in the United States and other countries.

Other company, product, and service names may be trademarks or service marks of others.

Preface

This IBM Redbook illustrates the architectural choices you have when designing an information technology (IT) infrastructure with IBM WebSphere® Application Server for z/OS® and one or more back-end systems. This book shows you the pros and cons of using WebSphere Application Server with CICS®, IMS™, IBM WebSphere MQ and DB2®.

Actually a presentation guide you can use, this redbook comes with presentation foils included in the additional material. This material helps clients, potential clients and IBM staff to visualize high-level solutions. For each connectivity choice we discuss these attributes:

- Performance
- Security
- Availability
- Transactional capabilities
- Scalability

This book is based on the work of a group of leading-edge IBM @server® zSeries® customers and IBM experts known as the zSeries Business Leadership Council.

The team that wrote this redbook

This redbook was produced by a team of specialists from around the world working at the International Technical Support Organization, Poughkeepsie Center.

Tamas Vilaghy is a project leader at the International Technical Support Organization (ITSO), Poughkeepsie Center. He leads redbook projects about e-business on zSeries servers. Before joining the ITSO, he worked in the System Sales Unit and Global Services departments of IBM Hungary. Tamas spent two years in Poughkeepsie from 1998 to 2000 dealing with zSeries marketing and competitive analysis. From 1991 to 1998 he held technical, marketing and sales positions for zSeries. From 1979 to 1991 he dealt with system software installation, development and education.

Mariangela Cecchetti is an IT Specialist in IBM z/Series Server Group, Italy. She has three years of experience in WebSphere for zSeries field. Her areas of expertise include installation, configuration, and administration of WebSphere for z/OS. She holds a degree in Information Science from the Univeristà di Pisa.

Mitch Johnson is a Consulting IT Specialist in IBM Software Services for WebSphere (ISSW) at IBM's Research Triangle Laboratory, North Carolina. His areas of expertise include enterprise connectivity and installation, configuration, and administration of WebSphere for z/OS and IMS as well as CICS, TXSeries®, and DB2 on various platforms. He holds a Bachelor of Science in Computer Science from North Carolina State University in Raleigh, NC

Frank P Jones is a Certified Consulting IT Specialist for zSeries WebSphere in New York. He has spent over 23 years at IBM and has held a number of different field, headquarters and development positions. His areas of expertise include system integration, performance and telecommunication systems. Over the last several years, he has worked as a WebSphere Host Integration IT Specialist, Architect and Project Manager for HVWS for performance testing and as a Client IT Architect. He was Chairman of the New York IEEE Communications Society and still serves on the executive board. He holds an MA degree in Mathematics from NYU Courant Institute of Mathematical Sciences and a BS degree in Economics from CCNY.

John Kettner is a Consulting IT Architect in zSeries Advanced Architecture Support (AAS). He has 28 years in the IT industry. Previous to AAS, he was the IT Specialist for Websphere on z/OS in the Americas North East. Prior to IBM, he worked on Wall Street in senior IT management positions and has a degree in Computer Science.

Fabio Riva is a IT Architect in IBM Global Services in Italy. He has 19 years of experience in the various mainframe fields. In recent years, his focus has been on the preparation of cost-effective solutions for IBM IGS Outsourcing zSeries Customers, and in the development and proposal of strategic solutions using new technology such as Java™, WebSphere and Linux, in order to access mainframe data. His areas of expertise include the development and proposal of other types of cross-platform solutions, such as SAP R/3 databases on zSeries with application servers in open environments.

Thanks to the following people for their contributions to this project:

Patrick C. Ryan, Rica Weller
ITSO Center, IBM Poughkeepsie

Thomas Hackett
IBM New Technology Center, Poughkeepsie

Leigh Compton, Judy Ruby-Brown, Suzie Wendler, Kenneth R. Blackman
IBM Advanced Technical Support

Ivan Joslin
IBM WebSphere Development, Poughkeepsie

Mike Cox
IBM Washington Systems Center

Alberto Cesarini, Claudio Scarabotta
IBM Global Services SO Service Delivery, Perugia, Italy

Dermot Flaherty
IBM WebSphere MQ Hursley Lab, IBM UK

Betty Patterson, Haley Fung, Shyh-Mei Ho, Kyle Charlet, Judith Hill, Kevin Flanigan, Gerald Hughes
IBM IMS Santa Teresa Lab

Hilon Potter, Frank DeGilio
IBM Design Center for On Demand Business

Phil Wakelin
IBM Hursley CICS TG development, UK

Nigel Williams
IBM Montpellier, Design Center for On Demand Business

Become a published author

Join us for a two- to six-week residency program! Help write an IBM Redbook dealing with specific products or solutions, while getting hands-on experience with leading-edge technologies. You'll team with IBM technical professionals, Business Partners and/or customers.

Your efforts will help increase product acceptance and customer satisfaction. As a bonus, you'll develop a network of contacts in IBM development labs, and increase your productivity and marketability.

Find out more about the residency program, browse the residency index, and apply online at:

ibm.com/redbooks/residencies.html

Comments welcome

Your comments are important to us!

We want our Redbooks™ to be as helpful as possible. Send us your comments about this or other Redbooks in one of the following ways:

► Use the online **Contact us** review redbook form found at:

ibm.com/redbooks

► Send your comments in an Internet note to:

redbook@us.ibm.com

► Mail your comments to:

IBM® Corporation, International Technical Support Organization
Dept. HYJ Mail Station P099
2455 South Road
Poughkeepsie, NY 12601-5400

Architectural considerations

In this chapter we introduce the topics and factors which must be considered when connecting to an Enterprise Information System (EIS) or database (DB) from WebSphere on z/OS.

> **Attention:** These considerations assume applications are well-designed and were developed using current application development best practices.

In this chapter we compare and contrast:

- Synchronous and asynchronous connections
- Local and remote connections

The following attributes are discussed for the different connections:

- Performance
- Availability
- Scalability
- Security
- Transactional capabilities
- Other issues

© Copyright IBM Corp. 2004. All rights reserved.

1.1 The connectivity conundrum

- Many choices to connect WebSphere to EIS's and DBs:
  - Local v. Remote
  - Synchronous v. Asynchronous
- Different connectivity attributes:
  - Performance
  - Availability
  - Security
  - Transactionality
  - Scalability
  - Other issues, drawbacks
- What to choose under which circumstances ?
- Architectural perspectives and practices.

Figure 1-1 The conundrum of choices

Connecting to an EIS or DB raises numerous questions and issues, as in Figure 1-1, that need to be addressed:

▶ Is the flow the sending of a request followed by a receiving of results, *synchronous*?

▶ Does the flow consist of series of sends and receives in no particular order, *asynchronous*?

▶ Is the target of the request collocated with WebSphere, or is it remote?

▶ What are my performance expectations?

▶ What are my availability requirements?

▶ What security or protection do I need to include with my request?

▶ What are my plans for handling growth?

1.2 The first decision point

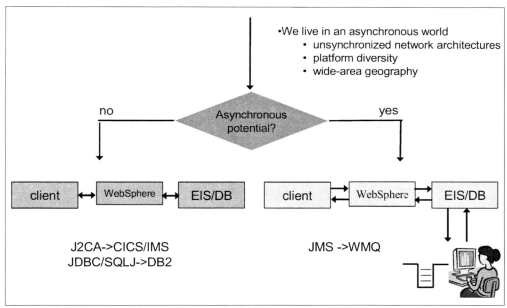

Figure 1-2   The first decision point

The first decision point is based on the nature of the back-end, or target Enterprise Information System (EIS) application. See Figure 1-2. Customer Information Control System (CICS), Information Management System (IMS), and DB2 are traditionally synchronous. A request is sent from a client, such as WebSphere, and the results are returned before the client proceeds.

WebSphere MQSeries® is asynchronous, a message is sent and WebSphere MQSeries does not need to wait for the results. A recent Gartner study mentions that more and more asynchronous communication will occur in the Web services arena, eventhough Web services started as a synchronous way of communicating.

1.3 Asynchronous versus synchronous

- Performance of Asynchronous
  - ▸ Is likely not to be as good as synchronous
- Availability of Asynchronous
  - ▸ Is slightly better than synchronous
- Scalability of Asynchronous
  - ▸ Is comparable with synchronous
- Security with Asynchronous
  - ▸ Is not as robust since identity is not passed automatically
- Transactionality with Asynchronous
  - ▸ Is supported only for initial queuing of message, not end-to-end

Figure 1-3   Asynchronous versus synchronous attributes comparisons

If you have a choice, there are several attributes of asynchronous (ASYNC) and synchronous (SYNC) connectivity which must be considered and compared. Figure 1-3 is a good overview of the attributes of ASYNC. Each situation is different. Its requirements must be evaluated to determine the best solution.

For each client situation, multiple attributes influence the decision whether to use SYNC or ASYNC.

If performance is a major issue, choose SYNC. If availability is a major issue, choose ASYNC, because the message queuing systems guarantee message delivery. If security is a major issue, choose SYNC, as the security propagation and trust is more developed in that case. If you need end-to-end transactions, then definitely the SYNC communication is the way to go.

Try to analyze the business functional and non-functional requirements and come up with a good balance of solutions to the requirements.

1.4 Asynchronous transactions: A developer's view

- Application developers want a "synchronous" view partly because users have a "synchronous" view
  - processes share same fate or outcome
  - all must succeed for any to succeed
  - if one fails, all should fail

- Delivering a synchronous solution may be difficult/impossible
  - exploit synchronous solutions where it's possible
  - don't pretend it's possible where it's not
  - two different perspectives forced on app. developer

Figure 1-4 A developer's view

See Figure 1-4. A synchronous solution is much easier for an application programmer for the following reasons:

- Results are available immediately.
- Error handling is much easier.
  - Soft errors, such as a record not found or an invalid request, can be addressed in the same code which made the original request.
  - Hard errors, such as communication problems which may cause exceptions, can be handled immediately.

However, in a lot of cases the choice to select asynchronous or synchronous connectivity is limited by the circumstances. The most important issue is not to force an asynchronous solution to a synchronous problem. The reverse is also true.

Chapter 1. Architectural considerations   **5**

1.5 z/OS concepts and terminology

Before we proceed, you need to be aware of some terms and definitions. These will be used in figures and explanations in this and subsequent chapters.

See Figure 1-5. These acronyms refer to various z/OS terms, components or concepts that are a part of following discussions about connectivity options and attributes. See "Abbreviations and acronyms" on page 143 for more information about the terms used in this book.

---

* zSeries hardware allows the allocation of resources to multiple logical partitions (**LPARs**) within a single zSeries machine, with each partition supporting a single operating system image.

* A **SYSPLEX** is a collection of LPARs joined together to form a single logical entity or view to an external observer

* A Cross Coupling Facility (**XCF**) is a zSeries machine with microcode that allows high speed communications between LPARs in a SYSPLEX and well as a common repository for sharing data by subsystems like IMS and DB2 that are in different LPARs in the SYSPLEX.

* Resource Recovery Services (**RRS**) is a z/OS component which can perform transaction management for multiple subsystems (CICS,DB2, IMS, WebSphere, WMQ) on the same LPAR.

* Workload Manager (**WLM**) uses installation defined policies and service level commitments to govern the performance (response time, etc.) of work within the system.

* Dynamic Virtual IP Address (**DVIPA**) is a common external IP address for an application residing or executing on different LPARs in the SYSPLEX.

* Sysplex Distributor (**SD**) is a z/OS component (part of the TCP/IP stack) which uses WLM to distribute inbound DVIPA requests to the LPAR in the SYPSLEX best able to handle the work.

* Resource Control Access Facility (**RACF**) is a security manager.

* Automatic Restart Management (**ARM**) is a z/OS component which will try to restart a job or task after a failure.

Figure 1-5   z/OS concepts and terms

6   WebSphere for z/OS Connectivity Architectural Choices

1.6 WebSphere concepts and terminology

In Figure 1-6, these terms refer to WebSphere components or concepts used to describe the various connectivity options and attributes.

---

* A **Server** is comprised of a *controller* region and one are more *servant* regions.

* A **Node** is a collection or set of *servers* on a given system or logical partition (LPAR).

* A **Cell** is a collection or set of *nodes* that make up an administrative domain.

* A Resource Adapter (**RA**) is code (Java JARs, native executables) supplied by an EIS vendor to be installed in a WebSphere Server in order to provide access to the vendor's EIS or DB system.

* An alias for a customized Java Authentication and Authorization (**JAAS**) login module can be specified in the **Mapping Configuration Alias** of a JCA Connection Factory. A customized JAAS login module can be used to provide an alternate resource principle to an EIS/DB.

* When **Container-managed** authentication is specified, the user ID and optional password used on the connection are provided by the container either by the JCA connection factory or the Container-managed Authentication Alias entry.

* When **Application-managed** authentication is specified, the user ID and password used on the connection are provided explicitly by the application or the Component-managed Authentication Alias entry.

Figure 1-6   WebSphere concepts and terms

1.7 Transaction management concepts and terminology

The acronyms and terms in Figure 1-7 define transaction management terms or concepts. For more information refer to redpaper *Transactions in J2EE* REDP-3659-00.

- A *Local transaction* is when there is one resource manager controlling all the changes made within the scope of a transaction.

- A *Global transaction* is when multiple resource managers are involved in the scope of a transaction.

- *2PC* (Two Phase Commit) is a 2 part series of actions which ensures that either all changes made to multiple resource managers are committed or all changes made to multiple resource managers are rolled back. The first phase tells each resource manager to prepare to commit. When positive responses have been received from each resource manger, the second phase tells them to commit the changes.

- The alternative is *1PC* where there is no prepare phase and therefore no opportunity to recover if a failure occurs during the commit process.

- *XA* refers to the X/Open distributed transaction processing (DTP) open standard implementation of 2PC processing for the coordinating of changes to multiple distributed relational databases and other resource managers which support the XA interface.

- Last Participant Support (*LPS*) refers to the scenario where a transaction manager coordinates a global transactions involving any number of 2PC capable resource managers and a single 1PC

Figure 1-7   Transaction management concepts and terms

The most-used term for transactions is ACID, defining the basic attributes of a transaction:

- *Atomicity*: A transaction should be done or undone completely. In the event of a failure, all operations and procedures should be undone, and all data should roll back to its previous state.

- *Consistency*: A transaction should transform a system from one consistent state to another consistent state.

- *Isolation*: Each transaction should happen independently of other transactions occurring at the same time.

- *Durability*: Completed transactions should remain permanent, even during system failure.

1.8 WebSphere for z/OS clustering

This section explains some additional WebSphere topology information:

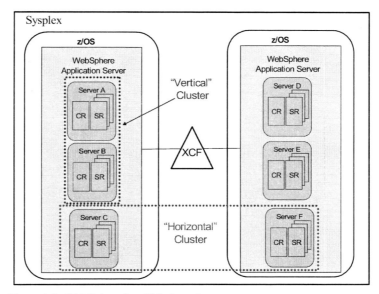

Figure 1-8   WebSphere for z/OS clustering

A *cluster* is a grouping of two or more servers into a single logical entity, primarily for administrative purposes. See Figure 1-8. Applications are installed into a cluster, meaning the application is deployed into all of the servers in that cluster.

Clusters can be *horizontal* across multiple logical partitions (LPARs), or they can be *vertical*, with all of the servers on the same LPAR.

Note: Resources such as real memory or processors limit the number of servers which should be added in a vertical cluster.

1.9 WebSphere for z/OS failover and load-balancing

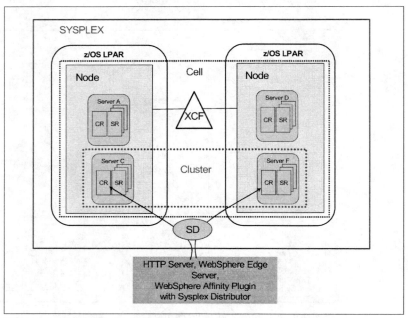

Figure 1-9   Failover and load balancing

Various products and solutions allow the distribution, or *balancing*, of work across the servers in a cluster, as in Figure 1-9. When an outage occurs at the LPAR or server level, these same products prevent the disruption of new work requests.

For more information see *Enabling High Availability eBusiness on zSeries - SG24-6850-01*

1.10 Types of WebSphere connections

> ▪ A **Local Connection** is when the WebSphere server and the EIS/DB are on the same LPAR and communications between the two is done using cross memory services or other non-network facilities.
>
> ▪ A **Remote Connection** is when the WebSphere server and the EIS/DB communications between the two is done using TCP/IP. (It is a remote connection even if the two endpoints are on the same LPAR as long as communications is done by TCP/IP).

Figure 1-10   Types of WebSphere connections

In Figure 1-10, there are two types of connections from WebSphere to an EIS or DB:

- ► A *local* connection means WebSphere accesses an EIS or DB on the same LPAR using cross-memory services.
- ► A *remote* connection means WebSphere accesses an EIS or DB using a network.

In the distributed WebSphere world connections are always remote, using TCP/IP. WebSphere for z/OS has a set of J2CA connectors that were developed to use local, memory-to-memory communication between WebSphere and the EIS systems. The tight integration between WebSphere and EIS results in better performance and security.

Chapter 1. Architectural considerations   **11**

1.11 Local connections

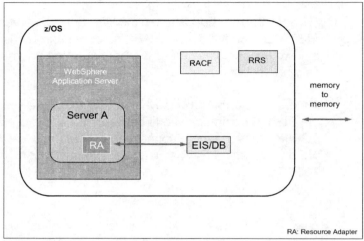

Figure 1-11   Local connection

Local connections are on the same node, or LPAR, as the WebSphere server. See Figure 1-11. This is desirable for a number of reasons:

- No inherent network delay because the request is not impacted by any overhead required to use network facilities
- More options for the server on the identity are passed to the EIS or DB for authorization
- Transaction control management by Resource Recovery Services (RRS) is available

The WebSphere server, the local EIS/DB and the LPAR are all single points of failure. If one fails, then, to a client, it appears that there is total failure.

1.11.1 Local connection: Attributes

- **Performance**
  - Is good since there is no network delay

- **Availability**
  - Is good as long as WebSphere and the target EIS/DB are both available

- **Scalability**
  - Is available only by adding additional servers

- **Security**
  - Is able to use the thread identity or RUNAS value as the connection identity

- **Transactionality**
  - 2PC is supported when all resource managers are RRS enabled

Figure 1-12   Local connection attributes

A local connection is defined as the WebSphere server and the EIS or DB being located on the same LPAR, and cross-memory services or other non-network facilities, are used for communications. Figure 1-12 lists the attributes of a local connection.

The performance is the best in this case, as network delay can be avoided with memory-to-memory communication. We run WebSphere and the EIS in the same LPAR and we have one instance of each. As a result, availability is limited to each component's availability.

You can assign multiple processors and more memory to a given LPAR to increase scalability, but the resources are still limited to the one LPAR.

Security is the best in the local case. Local connectors assume trust, no possibility of a network attack, so the EIS system uses the thread identity support.

Chapter 1. Architectural considerations   **13**

1.12 Remote connections

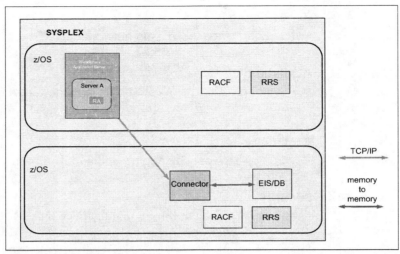

Figure 1-13   Remote connections

It is possible to isolate WebSphere from the production EIS by moving it to another LPAR. However, you run into several issues:

- This adds the overhead of network delay to the request.
- Thread identity and RUNAS are not available for the use as the connection identity.
- Two-phase commit (2PC) of a global transaction is not always available.

Figure 1-13 is an example of isolation. The WebSphere server and the EIS/DB are still single points of failure. If either has a failure, then all work ceases.

1.12.1 Remote connection: Attributes

* **Performance**
  - Can be adversely affected by any network delay
* **Availability**
  - The restarts are faster, less components to restart
  - If multiple LPARs are used, better availability
* **Scalability**
  - Is easier since options like using Sysplex Distributor are available
* **Security**
  - Does not offer as many options for connection identities
* **Transactionality**
  - Can be limited in circumstances when transactions span multiple LPARs

Figure 1-14   Remote connection attributes

A remote connection is when communication between the WebSphere server and the EIS/DB use TCP/IP for communications. See Figure 1-14.

The remote case involves the use of network protocols. On both LPARs, the network layers are involved and there is more overhead compared to local communications.

Availability
Availability depends on the number of WebSphere and EIS LPARs, and the workload-balancing and distribution mechanism used in the topology.

Security
Security is determined by the use of TCP/IP network protocol. User ID and password need to be specified for the EIS to do authentication.

Transactional capabilities
Transactional capabilities are dependent on the availability characteristics. The use of a sysplex distributor limits the recovery capability of transactions.

Chapter 1. Architectural considerations   **15**

1.13 Local connection with some availability

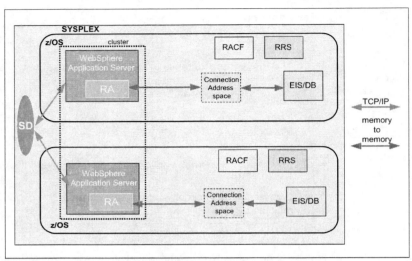

Figure 1-15 Local connection with some availability

We can duplicate the local configuration and remove the single point of failure. See Figure 1-15. However, a single point of failure still exists with the EIS or DB. If they are not available, there is no way Workload Manager (WLM) knows before work is scheduled for a particular WebSphere server. This work quickly fails and WLM assumes this server is a good place to send additional work. This additional work fails and continues driving more and more work to this WebSphere server, creating what is known as a *storm drain* scenario.

> **Note:** Sysplex Distributor is used only on the first inbound request. Once a Server is selected and the proper JSESSIONID has been stored in the HTTP cookie, all subsequent requests bypass Sysplex Distributor and are routed directly to the original server by WebSphere's HTTP plug-in. See *Enabling High Availability eBusiness on zSeries* - SG24-6850-01 for more information.

1.14 Remote connection with availability

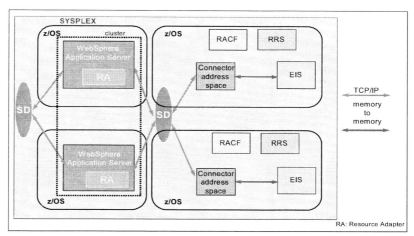

Figure 1-16   Remote connection with availability

If we change the EIS/DB local connections to remote connections and use Sysplex Distributor to route the request, we have removed WebSphere and the EIS/DB as single points of failure. There is redundancy for each component. See Figure 1-16.

But at what cost to the connection attributes for a specific EIS or DB? The answer to this question and other factors are provided in subsequent chapters for EIS and DB.

> **Important:** The transaction cannot be recovered if the sysplex distributor is between WebSphere and the connector address spaces. The reason is that the sysplex distributor might route the recovery request to a different connector address space.

18   WebSphere for z/OS Connectivity Architectural Choices

2

DB2 connectivity options

This chapter provides topology options for connecting WebSphere Application Server on a z/OS to DB2 subsystem.

In this chapter, we discuss the following topics:

- ► How to access DB2 from a Java program
- ► Java database connectivity (JDBC) driver types
- ► Considerations on connectivity attributes in local and remote scenarios:
  - Performance
  - Availability
  - Security
  - Transactional capabilities
  - Scalability

© Copyright IBM Corp. 2004. All rights reserved.

19

2.1 Accessing DB2 from a Java program

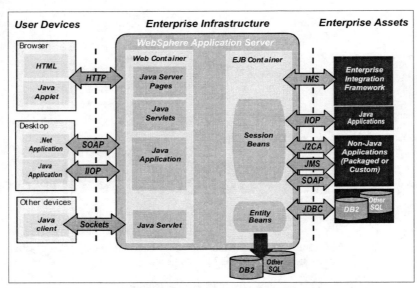

Figure 2-1   Inbound and outbound access to/from WebSphere

When accessing relational data from a Java application, you first need to understand Java Database Connectivity (JDBC). All database access occurs through JDBC, from connecting to a database to processing the data in that database. See Figure 2-1.

JDBC is an application programming interface (API) that the Java programming language uses to access different forms of tabular data, as well as some hierarchical systems. The list includes full-blown relational databases such as DB2, down to spreadsheets and flat files. The JDBC specifications were developed by Sun Microsystems, Inc. together with relational database providers, such as IBM and Oracle, to ensure the portability of Java applications across databases and platforms. At this time, there have been three major releases of the JDBC API specification. The last one is JDBC 3.0, which was released in February 2002.

An interface is a Java construct that looks like a class but does not provide an implementation of its methods. In the case of JDBC, the actual implementation of the JDBC interfaces is provided by the database vendor as a JDBC driver.

This might sound complex, but it provides portability. All access using JDBC is through standard calls with standard parameters. This means an application can be coded with little regard to the database you are actually using, because all the platform-dependent code is stored in the JDBC drivers.

JDBC also has to be flexible in what functionality it does and does not provide, solely based on the fact that different database systems have different levels of functionality. For example, JDBC provides a method called getArray(), which supports a column-type of array. This column type is not supported by DB2, and therefore such a function is meaningless. When a DBMS does not support such functions, the JDBC standard says that if the method is executed in a program, the driver has to raise an SQLException.

Although JDBC allows for greater portability, it is important to understand what functionality is available in the database system that you are using. On the other hand, the vendors that provide JDBC drivers can add functionality that is database system-specific. These methods are known as extensions. Although they can provide benefits, they should also be used carefully, because they limit portability.

2.2 JDBC driver types

As was mentioned before, the JDBC drivers provide the physical code that implements the objects, methods, and data types defined in the JDBC specification. The JDBC standard defines four different types of drivers, numbered 1 to 4. See Figure 2-2. The distinction between them is based on how the driver is physically implemented, and how it communicates with the database.

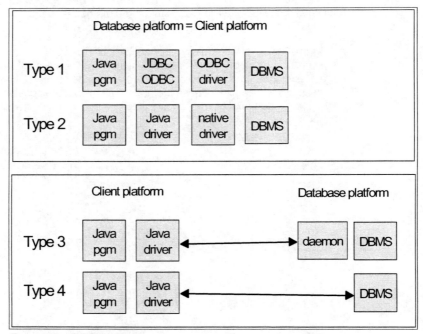

Figure 2-2   JDBC driver types

> **Note:** The naming of these driver types does not represent improvements or versioning of the drivers. Type 2 drivers are not a later version than Type 1 drivers. Type 4 is not a fuller implementation of a standard than a Type 2 driver.

The following sections describe the four driver types in detail.

2.2.1 Type 1

Type 1 (T1) is the oldest driver type. It was provided by Sun to promote JDBC when no database-specific drivers were available. With this driver, the JDBC API calls an open database connectivity (ODBC) driver to access the database. This driver is commonly referred to as a *JDBC-ODBC bridge* driver. It is no longer commonly used. Virtually every database vendor today supports JDBC and provides their own, vendor-specific driver. For DB2, T1 is not officially supported.

2.2.2 Type 2

In a Type 2 (T2) driver, the JDBC API calls platform- and database-specific code to access the database. This is the most common driver, and offers the best performance. However, because the driver code is platform-specific, a different version has to be coded by the database vendor for each platform.

2.2.3 Type 3

With Type 3 (T3), the JDBC API calls are routed through a middle ware product using standard network protocols such as TCP/IP. The driver itself is written in Java.

The middle ware translates these calls into database-specific calls to access the target database and returns data to the calling application. In the case of DB2, this task is performed by a program called the JDBC applet server. DB2 for z/OS and OS/390® do not supply a T3 driver.

2.2.4 Type 4

A Type 4 (T4) driver is fully written in Java. It accesses the target database directly using the protocol of that database. In DB2, this is Distributed Relational Database Architecture™ (DRDA®). As the driver is fully written in Java, it can be ported to any platform that supports that DBMS protocol without change, allowing applications to use it across platforms.

IBM provides the T4 driver through a no-charge, optional feature of DB2 Universal Database™ Server for z/OS and OS/390 Version 7 and later. This feature is the DB2 Universal Database Driver for z/OS, Java Edition. DB2 Universal Database Driver for z/OS, Java Edition provides a T4 JDBC connectivity that supports two-phase commit. This is sometimes called the *T4-XA (Extended Architecture)* driver. Java applications running inside the WebSphere Application Server talk to the universal T4 JDBC driver that supports two-phase commit, and the driver talks directly to the remote database server through DRDA. The universal T 4 driver implements DRDA Application Requester functionality.

Chapter 2. DB2 connectivity options **23**

2.3 Connecting from WebSphere to DB2 on z/OS

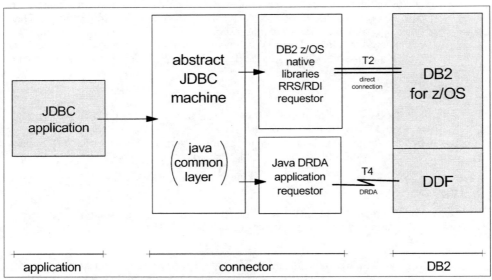

Figure 2-3   JDBC drivers for z/OS

In order to access DB2 UDB for OS/390 or z/OS, IBM provides a T2 driver and a driver that combines T2 and T4 JDBC implementations. See Figure 2-3. A short description of T2 and T4 JDBC implementations follows:

- DB2 Universal JDBC Driver for z/OS

  The DB2 Universal JDBC Driver is a single driver that includes JDBC T2 and JDBC T4 behavior, as well as Structured Query Language for Java (SQLJ) support. When an application loads the DB2 Universal JDBC Driver, a single driver instance is loaded for T2 and T4 implementations. The application can make T2 and T4 connections using this single driver instance. The connections can be made concurrently for both types. DB2 Universal JDBC Driver T2 behavior is referred to as DB2 Universal JDBC Driver T2 connectivity. DB2 Universal JDBC Driver T4 behavior is referred to as DB2 Universal JDBC Driver T4 connectivity.

- Legacy JDBC Type 2 driver for DB2 for z/OS

  The JDBC/SQLJ 2.0 Driver for OS/390 is a T2 driver that contains most of the functions that are described in the JDBC 1.2 specification. This driver also includes some of the functions that are described in the JDBC 2.0 specification. This is the Legacy DB2 for z/OS Local JDBC T2 compliant driver that has been available since the first release of WebSphere Application Server 5.0 for z/OS. This driver supports two-phase commit processing.

In general, use JDBC T2 connectivity for Java programs that run on the same z/OS system with the target DB2 subsystem on the same LPAR. Use JDBC T4 connectivity from Java programs accessing target DB2 subsystems on different z/OS systems.

If you need two-phase commit processing (2PC) on JDBC T4 connections, you need a particular JDBC T4 driver, Type 4-XA.

WebSphere Application Server V5 for z/OS is the first level to offer three DB2 JDBC Providers, selectable from an Administrative Console panel. Earlier levels of WebSphere Application Server 5.0 offer only the DB2 for z/OS Local JDBC Provider (RRS). The JDBC providers included in WebSphere V5 are:

► DB2 for z/OS Local JDBC Provider (RRS)

This is the Legacy DB2 for z/OS Local JDBC type-2 compliant provider that has been available for a long time, also in WebSphere V4. This provider supports two-phase commit processing using Resource Recovery Services (RRS).

► DB2 Universal JDBC Driver Provider

This is the J2EE non-XA DB2 Universal JDBC Driver-compliant provider. This provider can be used with a JDBC T2 or T4 driver. When used with a T2 driver, two-phase commit processing is provided by RRS. When used with a T4 driver, two-phase commit processing is not available.

► DB2 Universal JDBC Driver Provider (XA)

This is the J2EE XA DB2 Universal JDBC Driver-compliant provider. This provider can be used only with a JDBC T4 driver. Datasources created under this provider support the use of J2EE XA protocol to perform two-phase commit processing. Use of a JDBC Type 2 driver on WebSphere Application Server for z/OS is not supported for datasources created under this provider.

The JDBC Provider and JDBC Driver that are being used are selected by using the WebSphere Application Server 5.0 Administrative panels. In these panels, you have to define the datasources, the JDBC driver and the associated JDBC provider.

Chapter 2. DB2 connectivity options   **25**

2.4 Different connectivity scenarios

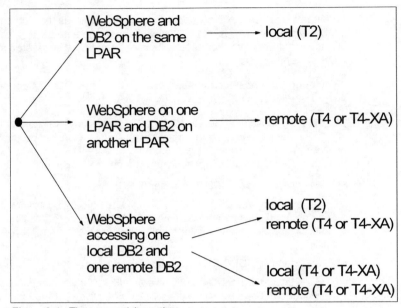

Figure 2-4   The connectivity options

Because the topic of JDBC drivers is complex, it is useful to show these concepts using concrete connectivity scenarios. See Figure 2-4. In the following sections, we analyze the following situations:

- WebSphere and DB2 on the same LPAR

  See 2.5, "Local DB2 connection" on page 27.

- WebSphere on one LPAR and DB2 on another

  See 2.6, "Remote DB2 connection" on page 30.

- WebSphere accessing both a local DB2 and a remote DB2

  See 2.7, "Mixed DB2 configuration: local T2 and remote T4" on page 33.

We discuss the pros and cons of these connectivity scenarios to better understand the implications of each architectural choice.

2.5 Local DB2 connection

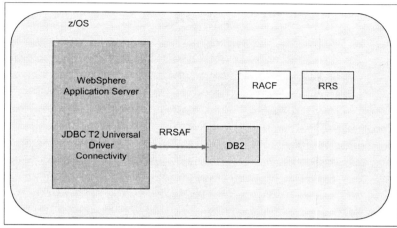

Figure 2-5   Connecting to local DB2

A local connectivity scenario, as in Figure 2-5, represents the simplest way to connect WebSphere application to DB2 on z/OS. The application and the DB2 subsystem run on the same LPAR. Because the application is local to the DBMS, the best way to access DB2 data is using a T2 driver that can do native calls to DB2. This configuration normally provides the best performance.

In this configuration, the Java application talks to DB2 through a T2 driver. A JDBC call is translated by the T2 driver into SQL statements, and executed through the RRS attachment facility (RRSAF) by DB2. RRS provides two-phase commit processing.

In theory, it is possible to also use a T4 driver to connect to a local DB2 for z/OS and OS/390 subsystem through Distributed Relational Database Architecture (DRDA) and a distributed data facility (DDF). This is not a recommended setup for a production environment though, because all SQL requests go through DRDA over TCP/IP (through the TCP/IP stack) into DB2's DDF address space.

Eventhough DRDA is a very efficient database communication protocol, it is normally more expensive than going through the local RRS attachment.

As the functionality of the Universal Driver is almost identical for the T2 and T4 drivers from the application point of view, you only need to change the connection factory to switch between the driver types.

2.5.1 Local DB2 connection: Attributes

- **Performance**
  - Is good since there is no network delay
- **Availability**
  - As good as single z/OS image on a zSeries processor
- **Scalability**
  - As good as a single zSeries server can get
- **Security**
  - Is able to use the thread identity or RUNAS value as the connection identity
- **Transactionality**
  - Supports 2PC when all resource managers are RRS enabled

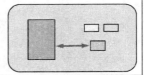

Figure 2-6   Local connection attributes

Performance

See Figure 2-6. From the performance point of view, the local connection with T2 driver has the best performance. There are no delays due to network connections, because all the actors of the connection reside on the same system and data movement is done at memory level.

The T2 JDBC driver is written partly in Java code and partly in native code. As a result, the performance is better with this configuration than with other types.

While there is also the possibility of using the T4-XA driver, this is not the suggested way to proceed. The performance is not as good as with a T2 driver, due to the additional path through the network layer.

Availability

From the availability point of view, having a single system means also having a single point of failure. No duplications in links, subsystems, connectors means lack of availability. In this configuration, availability is provided mainly by the traditional zSeries and z/OS availability.

Scalability

Scalability is acceptable. The local configuration lacks horizontal scalability because it is designed to satisfy the requirements related to a single installation. In order to scale the solution, additional instances should be used.

zSeries architecture ensures vertical scalability. You can increase the power of the server simply adding more processors to the LPAR.

Security

The level of security in this configuration is good, as the authorizations can be checked and passed at thread-level. In fact, in IBM WebSphere Application Server for z/OS there is a feature called Thread Identity support, which allows the current user identity assigned to the thread to be flowed to the EIS by the JDBC driver. The thread identity function is only available in those server configurations where J2CA connectors or JDBC providers access local z/OS resources through callable, not TCP/IP, interfaces.

See 2.13, "Security considerations for DB2 connections" on page 42, to obtain more details on this subject.

Transactional capabilities

The local configuration scenario allows the two-phase commit processing using the RRS facility. The DB2 subsystem uses RRS to coordinate resource commitment between DB2 and all other resource managers that also use RRS on a z/OS system. This guarantees a high level of transaction management, as for example, all the roll-back activities are automatically done by the subsystems.

2.6 Remote DB2 connection

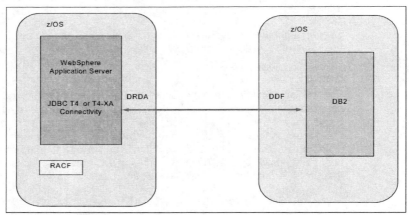

Figure 2-7   Remote connection

In certain businesses, security guidelines state that Web servers and the database server must not be on the same machine. These rules impose the use of two different LPARs separated by a firewall, one for Web serving and one for DB2, as in Figure 2-7.

Other businesses prefer to separate the newer LPARs from the traditional legacy environment, in order to reduce the total of cost of ownership. Using z/OS for a WebSphere LPAR does not affect legacy software costs, for example.

In this case we have to use a JDBC T4 or T4-XA driver to connect to DB2 on other LPARs. In Figure 2-7, both configurations are represented. The only difference between them is on the JDBC driver used (T4 or T4-XA).

It is possible to implement two-phase commit processing in the remote connection model, but in this case the use of JDBC T4-XA driver is required. JDBC T4-XA driver talks directly with the remote DB2 database server through DRDA.

Comparing this figure with the subsystem neutral version in Chapter 1, "Architectural considerations" on page 1, the connection address space for DB2 is integrated in the DB2 product.

2.6.1 Remote DB2 connection: Attributes

- **Performance**
  - Can be adversely affected by any network delay
- **Availability**
  - Is worse since we have two single points of failure. On the other hand if one system goes down, it may take shorter to restart.
- **Scalability**
  - Is easier, we can do vertical scaling independently on the two systems
- **Security**
  - Does not offer as many options for transferring identities
- **Transactionality**
  - Can be limited in circumstances when transactions span multiple LPARs

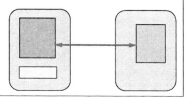

Figure 2-8   Remote connection attributes

Performance
From a performance point of view, a T4 connection does not perform as well as the local T2 connection. The reason for that is related to the additional path length required by the T4 connectivity in the network layer. Even if it can be improved by the use of zSeries facilities to reduce TCP/IP delays, the performance cannot beat the local connection with T2 driver. See Figure 2-8.

To realize two-phase commit processing you must use T4-XA. For single-phase commit, consider that performance between T4 and T4-XA are close. There is less then 1% of difference when 2PC is not used.

Availability
The level of availability is worse than the local connection. There are three single points of failure, the two systems and the single network connection. In the event one system fails, the restart time can be shorter compared to installing all software on a single system.

Scalability

Scalability is better than the local connection. The two systems can be scaled independently of each other, based on need.

Security

In remote connections, user ID and password credentials from container-managed or component-managed authentication aliases are used. A customized Java authentication and authorization services (JAAS) login module can also be used to specify the connection identity on remote connections. The connection identity can be the caller, the servant or the role identity, or any other identity the DB2 subsystem should use.

This is the standard way to control security in a distributed environment with J2EE Connector Architecture (J2CA) in order to access EIS.

See 2.12, "Security options" on page 40, for more information on this subject.

Transactional capabilities

With the T4 driver, no two-phase commit is available. In order to use 2PC, you need to use the T4-XA JDBC driver. The JDBC T4-XA driver talks directly with the remote DB2 database server through DRDA.

2.7 Mixed DB2 configuration: local T2 and remote T4

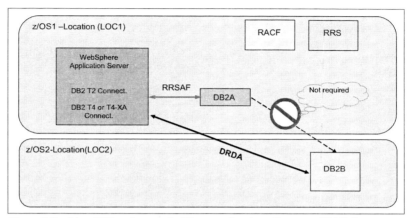

Figure 2-9 A local T2 and a remote T4 connection from the same WebSphere

In the previous sections we analyzed the different types of connections between WebSphere and DB2 subsystems. In most installations, the possible connections are not only local or remote. Most of the time, an application might access local data on a DB2 that resides on the same LPAR, plus other DB2 data that resides on other LPARs.

In this section, we analyze the scenario of one local and one remote DB2. See Figure 2-9. For local connections, the best choice is a T2 driver. It provides the best performance. The remote DB2 can be accessed with a T4 or T4-XA driver.

We start with the most commonly used configuration: Local T2 and Remote T4-XA. This kind of configuration can be used to access DB2 data within the same sysplex or outside it.

The z/OS system called LOC2 can be part of the sysplex or not.

Security

Security is managed at thread id level with the LOC1 system. This means that the Thread ID is passed to DB2 by the JDBC driver. The Security Authentication Facility (SAF) user ID is accepted by JDBC driver without re-authentication. The connection with the LOC2 system is managed with the Authentication Alias, either container-managed or component-managed. See Section 2.12, "Security options" on page 40 to obtain more details on this subject.

Transactional capabilities

Two-phase commit processing is supported by different actors in the different LPARS: 2PC is managed by WebSphere and RRS inside the LPAR called LOC1. With the LPAR called LOC2, 2PC is managed by WebSphere and by JDBC T4-XA driver directly.

There is no need to connect the distributed data facility (DDF) between the two DB2. We can use a direct T4-XA connection between WebSphere and the remote DB2.

As a variation to the previous solution, if you do not need 2PC transactions on both LPARs, you can use JDBC T2 for local connection, and JDBC T4 for remote connection.

Security

In this configuration, most of the information regarding the T2/T4-XA connection is still valid. This model can be used to access DB2 data in the same sysplex or outside, security is managed at Thread ID level with LOC1 system only, and it's possible to realize 2PC on LOC1 system using RRS facility. With LOC2, only one-phase commit (1PC) is possible.

2.8 Mixed DB2 configuration: Local and remote with the same T4 driver

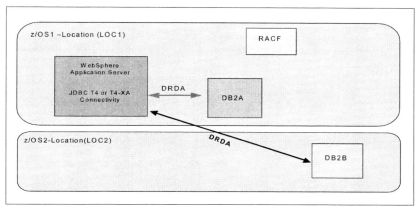

Figure 2-10 A local and a remote connection using T4 from the same WebSphere

Another possibility of a mixed configuration is to connect both the local DB2 and the remote DB2 with the same JDBC driver. See Figure 2-10. This is not the best way to proceed, as the performance of T2 in local connections is better then any T4 driver. The introduced delay is related to the additional path inside the network layer that a JDBC T4 driver should perform. At the same time, security is not as good with the T4 connectivity as with the T2.

This configuration is technically possible, and can be done using the same JDBC driver for both connections.

Using T4 driver, we can access DB2 data in local and remote DB2s that can be on the same sysplex or not. Two-phase commit processing is not available, as the JDBC driver is a T4, and the XA processing is needed for 2PC.

It's also possible to use a JDBC T4-XA driver, instead of a JDBC T4, to realize 2PC. Two-phase commit processing is managed by WebSphere and the JDBC T4-XA driver itself. The JDBC T4-XA driver talks directly with remote DB2 database server through DRDA.

2.9 Comparing DB2 performance

- For Local DB2, T2 gives best performance
  - T2 (RRS) is better than T4 XA – no trip through network layer

- When to use T4 vs. T4 XA? Remote DB2 - Choice is local vs global tran
  - Performance of both is close (1% if no 2PC processing is done)

- For multiple DB2s, choose the connectivity that give the best performance for each location (T2 for local, T4 for remote)
  - Application considerations? None, but deployer needs to know

- Universal Driver T2 performance equivalent to Legacy T2 driver

- SQLJ: Regarding connectivity the same applies as for JDBC
  - All arguments for SQLJ are still valid as for legacy case

Figure 2-11   Performance issues of the drivers

If you have to access a local DB2, the best way to get the best performance is using the JDBC T2 driver. See Figure 2-11. T2 connection is better then any T4 or T4-XA connections, because the movement of data is done at memory level, and there is no trip through the network layer. Using the T2 legacy driver or the T2 Universal Driver is the same, from the performance point-of-view.

To access remote DB2 without 2PC processing, you can use both T4 or T4-XA. The performance is very close, the difference in performances is around 1% without 2PC processing. To access remote DB2 with 2PC, you need T4-XA driver. In order to access multiple DB2 on different LPARs, choose the best suitable driver for each connection (T2 for local and T4 for remote).

2.10 Local DB2 with availability

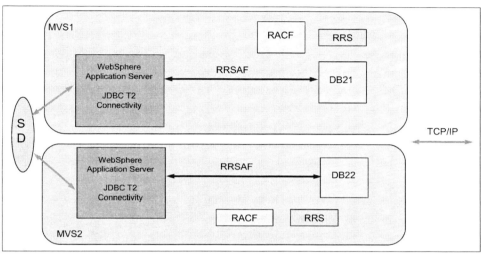

Figure 2-12   Local connection with availability

In local connections, we have to use one WebSphere application server in each LPAR. The Sysplex Distributor routes the request to one of the two application servers, and the Java application running inside WebSphere talks with DB2 using local connections. See Figure 2-12.

Using the DB2 data sharing feature, this configuration provides a good level of availability. WebSphere was removed as a single point of failure because they are duplicated. DB2 is duplicated and provides for availability, and, using data sharing, both of them can access the same DB2 data.

The main problem in this configuration comes from the connection between WebSphere and DB2. If the DB2 subsystem is not available, there is no way for WLM to know before work is scheduled to a particular WebSphere server. This work will quickly fail and WLM will assume this server is a good place to send additional work. This additional work will fail and continue to drive more and more work to this WebSphere server creating a storm drain.

This problem can be reduced if we use automation products to manage DB2 restart, and if we are able to automate the recycle of WebSphere connections. The JDBC T2 driver is able to reconnect to the same DB2 and purge the dead connections by itself.

Security is managed with thread identity facility, as all the actors are in the same LPAR (both WebSphere and DB2 are inside the same system).
Using this feature, the Java thread id authenticated by WebSphere is pushed to the OS thread, and the resource adapter uses it to access the DB2 subsystem. Please refer to Section 2.12, "Security options" on page 40 to obtain more details on this subject.

This configuration allows two-phase commit processing, using the RRS facility in each LPAR. DB2 subsystem uses RRS to coordinate resource commitment between DB2 and all other resource managers that also use RRS in the z/OS system.

2.11 Remote DB2 with availability

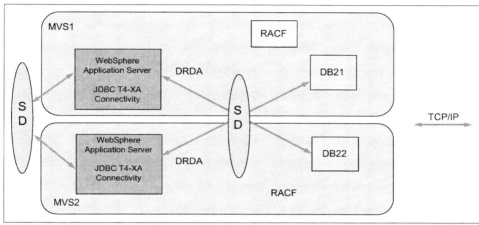

Figure 2-13   Remote connection with availability

In the remote case in Figure 2-13, we can cross the connections between WebSphere and DB2 on both LPARs. Removing the local connections (converting them to remote) and using the sysplex distributor can remove all single point of failures. This configuration has good availability.

On the other hand, this is not a suggested solution for DB2, due to the possibility of deadlock in global transactions. It is a possibility because Sysplex Distributor is only involved in getting a socket initially for a datasource connection. In a local transaction, each SQL statement executes on the same DB2, say DB21, because they are part of the same transaction and have the same connection.

However, when you have another data source going to the same database, and therefore, another connection, you can get routed to DB22 for that branch of the same transaction by Sysplex Distributor. You are then exposed to the possibility of deadlocks. That exposure can be mitigated by serially reusing the same connection. It is similar to using a local connection, but you lose the level of availability added by Sysplex Distributor.

To summarize, this configuration does provide maximum availability as long as you are not using global transactions.

However the local DB2 suffers in performance with T4 connectivity vs. T2 (about 50% worse). Why use the T4 driver if you are forced to use a local connection?

2.12 Security options

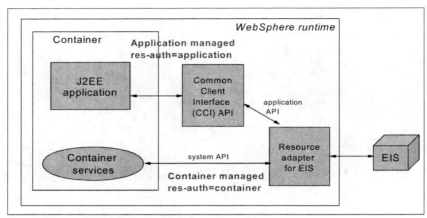

Figure 2-14   Security management options

Creating a new connection to an EIS requires a sign-on to EIS. In a managed environment as in the one provided by WebSphere, the J2EE security properties are used. The security manager component of WebSphere application server provides a secure access to EIS, in this case DB2. See Figure 2-14.

There are two standard ways by which a Java application requests a sign-on to an EIS:

- Container-managed (res-auth=container)

    The container (J2EE server) provides the security information to the resource adapter for EIS sign-on. The security information can be provided in the Datasource definition using the Authentication Alias to the J2EE server using the admin/deploy tool. For a local connection you can specify the Connection Manager RunAs Identity Enabled, that means the thread identity is passed to DB2.

- Component-managed (res-auth=application)

    The J2EE application provides security information to resource adapter for EIS sign-on. The security is provided in the application code via getConnection or in the Datasource definition using the Authentication Alias.

The deployer must set the security method in the deployment descriptor, giving a value to the res-auth element. The security information that is passed to the resource adapter is defined in the authentication alias, and consists of predefined use ID and password pairs, passed by the application or by J2EE server.

If WebSphere Application Server and the EIS system are running in the same LPAR (local configuration), there is the possibility to use a unique WebSphere for z/OS feature, called z/OS thread identity support. Using this feature, the Java thread id authenticated by WebSphere is pushed to the OS thread, and the resource adapter uses it to access DB2.

2.13 Security considerations for DB2 connections

- WebSphere, Universal Driver, DB2 in same z/OS image
  - Local option T2
  - Res-auth = container
  - Connection Manager RunAs Identity enabled
  - Run-as identity of the Java thread pushed to the OS thread when getting connection from UD
  - SAF userid accepted by Universal Driver without re-authentication
- Otherwise
  - For Res-auth = container, userid/password credential from container-managed authentication alias is defined in DataSource
  - For Res-auth = application, userid/password credential from application or from component-managed authentication alias
- Only one identity is passed
  - Based on Run-as (local), authentication alias or application
- No SSL – lightweight encryption only

Figure 2-15   Security options for WebSphere talking to DB2

As we discussed before, three ways of accessing a DB2 subsystem are available for a J2EE application running in WebSphere z/OS. The first one, unique for z/OS platform, uses the z/OS thread id support. This allows the use of the already SAF authenticated Java thread-id to access DB2 database, allowing high control in security and good performance, as there's no need for re-authentication. See Figure 2-15.

The other two ways to access DB2 are the standard methods defined in the J2EE security model. The access to DB2 is done by a JDBC driver using authentication aliases that will be re-authenticated by the driver itself, before accessing DB2. Authentication aliases are provided to JDBC driver either by the J2EE application (defined in the application code) or by the J2EE server (defined in the administration and deploy interface).

2.14 Migration from legacy JDBC driver to T2 UD

- No application changes needed
  - Application developer is not aware of whether it is a T4, T4 XA or T2
  - He just gets a DataSource, then gets a Connection
  - For deployed application, a new DataSource is defined, and the deployment descriptors are modified for WebSphere so the new driver is accessed
- WebSphere hides the complexity and just hands back the connection type specified in the deployment descriptor
- Legacy driver can't coexist in same WebSphere Application Server region with Universal driver
- Admin Panel > JDBC Providers > New Provider > you see the following choices
  1. **DB2 Universal JDBC Driver Provider** - if chosen, defaults to T4 and you must change it to T2 (RRS)
  2. **DB2 Universal JDBC Driver Provider (XA)**
  3. **DB2 for z/OS Local JDBC Provider (RRS)** – that is the Legacy driver

Figure 2-16   Migration issues from legacy to universal driver

The cornerstone for this solution is the DB2 Universal Java Client. It is a single JDBC (T2/T4) and SQLJ client for DB2 available in both workstation and z/OS configurations. Figure 2-16 explains the reason for making this choice. The DB2 Universal Java Client replaces individual clients under each configuration with a single product, making application behavior more portable across DB2 platforms. It improves DB2Connect consistency and performance by unifying many of the code paths for specific hardware configurations. For the enterprise application spread across many different hardware configurations, it is a single point of unification that the developer can count on, no matter the environment in which he or she works.

Migrating from the Legacy JDBC driver to the new Universal JDBC driver does not require application changes, as applications only get a Datasource and get a Connection. From the application point of view, having a T2, T4 or T4-XA connection is the same.

All the activities should be done at WebSphere level. From the Administrative Console panels you have to choose the correct JDBC provider, and select the corresponding possible JDBC drivers. In the figure you can see the providers

Chapter 2. DB2 connectivity options   **43**

available with WebSphere V5. Each of them has an associated JDBC driver. You must choose the right one for your type of connection (T2, T4 or T4-XA).

Migration can be performed in two ways:

- Defining a new WebSphere Application Server and reinstalling the applications.
  - Define a new WebSphere application server
  - Define the JDBC provider
  - Install existing applications without any change
- Switching the JDBC driver in existing WebSphere Application Server.
  - Test all applications within the application server with Universal Driver
  - Define new Datasources for all applications that run there
  - Stop and restart the Application Servers

There are three different ways to get the JDBC universal drive depending on the level of DB2 subsystem you have:

- DB2 for OS/390 V7 – FMID JDB7712, available as PTF PQ80841 (GA 3/2004)
  - T2, T4, T4-XA
- DB2 for z/OS V8 – FMID JDB8812, available as PTF PQ85053 (GA 3/2004)
  - T2, T4, T4 XA
- DB2 for OS/390 and z/OS V7/V8 – FMID HDDA210 (12/2003)
  - Called z/OS Application Connectivity to DB2 for z/OS and OS/390
  - For users that do not have a local DB2 with WebSphere
  - T4
  - T4 XA (for z/OS DB2 servers only)

2.15 SQLJ

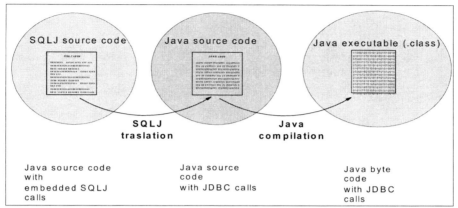

Figure 2-17   SQLJ processing

Structured Query Language for Java (SQLJ) complements and extends JDBC. See Figure 2-17. It enables quicker development cycles through a more concise syntax and safer code through much more extensive preexecution checking. In order to better understand how SQLJ complements JDBC, we briefly explain the difference between them.

DB2 provides a JDBC driver to support the basic functions of Java applications wanting to process relational data: establish a connection to a database, execute SQL requests, and process the results. The JDBC API consists of a set of classes and interfaces written in Java that provide a standard API for Java application developers to implement database applications. This API provides for portability across platforms and database systems. The value of the JDBC API is that an application can run on any platform with a Java Virtual Machine (JVM). The JDBC API only supports dynamic SQL, which means that its performance can benefit greatly from dynamic statement caching in the database engine. JDBC is defined as part of the J2EE platform or programming model.

The JDBC driver for DB2 also supports SQLJ. SQLJ, in contrast to JDBC, lets you write embedded SQL when developing Java applications. SQLJ was initially developed by a consortium of database vendors and has received wide database vendor acceptance: IBM, Oracle, Sybase, Informix®, and Compaq. Most importantly, the DB2 implementation of SQLJ provides support for true static SQL execution, which plays to the strengths of DB2 in terms of performance and security.

As does JDBC, SQLJ also provides for application portability across platforms and database systems, and SQLJ has been accepted as a standard by both ANSI and ISO. Currently, SQLJ is not part of the J2EE platform. IBM advocates for SQLJ to be included in the J2EE platform and the JDK. SQLJ parallels the JDBC model and covers all the basic functionality.

What are the advantages and disadvantages of using SQLJ vs. JDBC? There are strong compelling reasons for using SQLJ when developing enterprise class applications. For example, SQLJ is more concise and is less complex to code relative to JDBC. In Example 2-1 and Example 2-2, you can see the syntax differences:

Example 2-1   JDBC syntax

```
java.sql.PreparedStatement ps =
con.prepareStatement("SELECT ADDRESS FROM EMP
WHERE NAME=?");
ps.setString(1, name);
java.sql.ResultSet rs = ps.executeQuery();
rs.next();
addr = rs.getString(1);
rs.close();
```

Example 2-2   SQLJ syntax

```
#sql [con] { SELECT ADDRESS INTO :addr
FROM EMP
WHERE NAME=:name };
```

Another advantage is that all the SQL checking in terms of syntax and type mapping can be performed during program preparation instead of at run time. If DB2 has a customized version of the SQLJ profile, then SQLJ provides for static SQL execution, delivering better performance through reduced CPU resource consumption. This is because with static execution you avoid the full cost of prepare and run time checking.

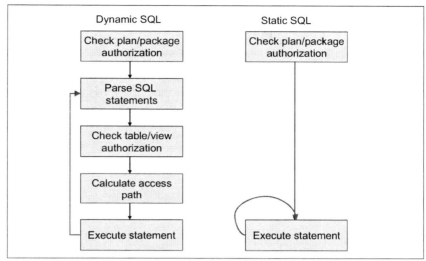

Figure 2-18 Static SQL versus dynamic SQL

SQLJ also delivers a tighter security authorization model because users are authorized to run programs and not to access the underlying tables. As a matter of fact, stronger security is the primary reason for customers to use SQLJ, followed closely by performance. As we continue to optimize the SQLJ implementation for improved price performance, the performance advantage of SQLJ over JDBC will become even more significant for our customers. In terms of positioning, SQLJ is also a strategic way to access relational data from Java applications. Figure 2-18 gives an overview of how optimized SQL delivers optimized performance.

Of course, an application does not always have to choose exclusively between SQLJ and JDBC. The JDBC driver lets you mix and match SQLJ and JDBC in the same application. SQLJ and JDBC can share the same JDBC connection. JDBC result sets can be turned into SQLJ iterators, and vice versa.

There are some cases where use of JDBC provides a better option. Some applications require the flexibility to build dynamically an SQL request at run time. For example, an application GUI may provide for selection from a large number of options. Coding a single SQLJ request to pull the qualifying rows may be lengthy, complex and may not optimize very well because the values of the host variables are not known until run time. It might be possible to code multiple different SQLJ requests, each of which can be executed on a best fit basis. However, this may lead to complex coding, and mileage may be limited. In such cases, the use of JDBC and dynamic SQL, and the ability to build up dynamically the SQL syntax may be a better option.

To read a deeper discussion on the subject of SQL, refer to chapter 5.2 of *DB2 UDB for z/OS Version 8: Everything You Ever Wanted to Know , ... and More,* SG24-6079.

3

CICS connectivity options

This chapter describes the different architectures to connect WebSphere Application Server for z/OS (WebSphere) to a CICS subsystem. Each architectural choice has its own unique attributes in performance, availability, security, transactional capabilities, scalability, plus other considerations. Many of the characteristics of these attributes have been discussed in "Architectural considerations" on page 1."

In this chapter, we build on this knowledge by discussing the major technology choices that are available today to connect to CICS from WebSphere. We present the different ways to connect WebSphere to CICS using technologies such as:

- ▶ CICS Transaction Gateway (CICS TG)

- ▶ Local WebSphere connection to CICS TG with an external CICS interface (EXCI) or Remote TCP/IP network connection

- ▶ Sysplex Distributor with Workload Manager (WLM) and Dynamic Virtual IP Address (DVIPA)

- ▶ CICSPlex® System Manager (SM)

- ▶ Direct connection through Remote Method Invocation (RMI) over Internet InterORB Protocol (IIOP)

- ▶ Simple Object Access Protocol (SOAP) for CICS feature

© Copyright IBM Corp. 2004. All rights reserved. **49**

3.1 CICS connection architectural choices

- **What are some of the WebSphere for z/OS connection choices to CICS?**
  - CICS Transaction Gateway (CICS TG)
    - Local option
    - Remote option
    - Variants of CICS TG using Sysplex Distributor and CICSPlex/SM
  - Connection using RMI/IIOP
  - SOAP connection

- **What are the different connectivity attributes for the above options?**
  - Performance
  - Availability
  - Security
  - Transactionality
  - Scalability

- **Which to choose under which circumstances?**

Figure 3-1 Architectural choices and their attributes

One key requirement for an architecture choice is the existing CICS infrastructure. The need to support this infrastructure moving forward, either for co-existence or migration, might drive you to a particular architecture decision. Figure 3-1 provides some questions to ask to help you arrive at your decision. While reviewing the architectural choices, it became clear to us that there were a number of approaches to designing a connection architecture:

1. Integrate CICS TG into WebSphere so the Resource Adapter (RA) accesses CICS in the same LPAR.

2. Use a resource adapter to connect to CICS TG through a network connection. This connection uses the ECI protocol over one of the remote protocols: TCP/IP, HTTP, Secure Sockets Layer (SSL) or HTTPS. The local or remote options have variants to increase availability and scalability.

3. Implement a J2EE container directly in CICS. This approach takes advantage of WebSphere Enterprise JavaBeans (EJB) to CICS EJB.

4. A SOAP server in CICS that lets a SOAP client invoke a CICS transaction using the SOAP server running within CICS.

These approaches have their own unique attributes that we describe in this chapter.

3.2 The resource adapter

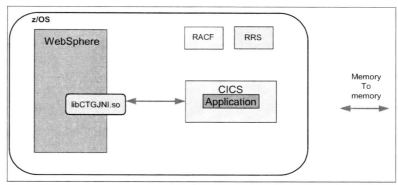

Figure 3-2   Interface components

The J2EE Connector Architecture (J2CA) specifies a standard way to access back-end Enterprise Information Systems (EIS) in the J2EE environment. Using J2CA, the application server communicates with EIS through a specific resource adapter, a connector that can be plugged into any application server. See Figure 3-2.

Each EIS vendor must provide a resource adapter that can be plugged into a J2CA-compliant application server. Resource adapters are provided by EIS vendors as *.rar (Resource Adapter Archive) files. Each resource adapter is specific to an EIS.

The specific *.rar file must be installed into IBM WebSphere Application Server for z/OS using the WebSphere console. The application server provides the infrastructure for connection, transaction, and security management.

The CICS resource adapter, which is supplied as part of the CICS Transaction Gateway (CICS RA or RA), not only implements the J2EE connector interface, but is RRS compliant. It is designed specifically to work with the RRS component of z/OS.

Resource recovery
Resource recovery consists of the protocols and program interfaces that allow WebSphere for z/OS and CICS to work together, making consistent changes to multiple, protected resources and participating in the two-phase commit process.

Transactional EXCI works together with z/OS RRS, and allows multiple EXCI calls to become part of one logical unit of work. This means that the CICS TG for z/OS can be used by other transactional systems such as WebSphere for z/OS to make transaction requests to CICS. This can be coordinated using a two-phase commit mechanism between the two systems.

EXCI requests can be transactional only if the address space using the EXCI and the CICS region execute in the same z/OS image. EXCI imposes this restriction.

Connection pooling

When retrieving data from an EIS, a large portion of the time is in the creation of the connection itself. Connection pooling alleviates this overhead. When you call for a connection, you are passed a handle to the next available connection that is in a ready-to-use state.

The CICS J2EE connectors result in a pool of connection objects instantiated inside the WebSphere Servant address space. This pool is created and controlled by the managed connection factory, the attributes of which are set during deployment of the CICS resource adapter. The pool increases performance greatly by removing the actual connection time. Scalability is handled by predefining as many connections in the pool as needed.

Thread Identity support in WebSphere and the flowed user ID

For security, the CICS resource adapter uses WebSphere Thread Identity. This is an important feature to understand when running WebSphere for z/OS and connecting to CICS.

WebSphere for z/OS V5 provides two unique features, Thread Identity and Thread Security, which can be exploited by J2CA-compliant resource adapters such as the CICS ECI resource adapter. The CICS ECI resource adapter does not use the Thread Security feature, but it does support Thread Identity.

Thread Identity support is used to flow the current thread identity to the back-end CICS. Most z/OS customers use this feature because it enables WebSphere for z/OS to behave in a way that traditional z/OS address spaces behave. That is, once you have authenticated, your user ID flows with any work you do within the z/OS system, cutting SMF audit trail records as it goes.

Thread Identity in WebSphere for z/OS applies only to container-managed connections. It allows the container to pass the security identity of the current Java thread to the J2CA connector and then to the CICS.

However, the user ID that the CICS ECI resource adapter flows to CICS is not always that of the current Java thread identity. Instead, it depends on several factors.

It is unlikely that you would connect a WebSphere node that had Global Security disabled to a CICS system that will usually have security enabled. Figure 3-3 illustrates the decision tree for most WebSphere for z/OS/CICS environments, where the ECI connection factory being used is configured in local mode and you are using a managed connection.

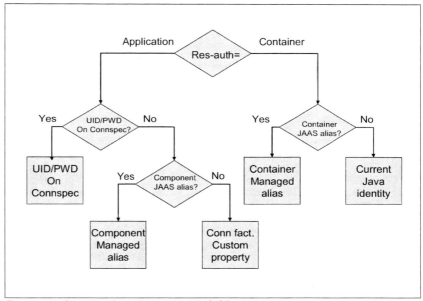

Figure 3-3   Security information used with CICS connection

Note that for res-auth=application, when no user ID is passed in the ConnectionSpec and there is no JAAS Component Alias defined, the flowed user ID is taken from the UserName custom property of the connection factory.

If you do not specify a UserName property on the connection factory, the flowed user ID defaults to the user ID of the WebSphere servant region when running in local mode, and to the user ID of the CICS TG daemon region when running in remote mode.

If the CICS TG daemon performs user ID and password checking (AUTH_USERID_PASSWORD=Yes), the request fails if no user ID or password is sent on the request.

For a full discussion on CICS Security, see *WebSphere Application Server for z/OS Version 5 and J2EE Security Handbook*, SG24-6086.

3.3 CICS Transaction Gateway

The CICS Transaction Gateway (CICS TG) is a set of client and server software components that allow an application such as an applet, a servlet, an enterprise bean, or any other application, to invoke services in a CICS region. The purpose of the CICS TG is to act as the link between the outside world, such as J2EE, and the world of CICS.

CICS supports two main protocols for communication between a client program and a CICS application, The External Presentation Interface (EPI) and the External Call Interface (ECI). ECI over TCP/IP is a communications mechanism that provides the connection from the CICS TG to a CICS region over an IP network. Using this protocol, you call a CICS program passing data and receiving response data in a COMMAREA.

The Gateway daemon is a long-running process that functions as a server to network-attached Java client applications, such as applets or remote applications, by listening on a specified TCP/IP port. In Local Mode, there is no CICS TG Daemon. In Remote Mode, there is a CICS TG Daemon address space on z/OS that listens to ECI requests from Java clients.

When you use the CICS TG on z/OS, only the ECI interface is supported. EXCI is a cross-memory implementation of ECI that is unique to z/OS.

The most common z/OS configuration makes use of a local CICS TG. On z/OS, this results in a direct cross-memory EXCI connection between the application server and CICS.

The CICS TG V5.01 introduced remote connection support, allowing a remote connection from the application server to a z/OS Gateway daemon. This functionality was introduced primarily for z/OS.e customers. z/OS.e is a specially priced offering of z/OS that provides select z/OS function for the zSeries 800 system. Traditional workloads, such as CICS Transaction Server (TS), are not licensed for z/OS.e. Because the CICS TG relies on the EXCI interface provided by CICS TS for z/OS, the CICS TG must be installed in a full-function z/OS LPAR. This means a remote connection must be used from WebSphere Application Server into the CICS TG.

The highest qualities of service, however, can be achieved when a local connection between the application server and the CICS region. In particular, this topology is the only topology that supports thread identity support and two-phase commit transactions.

54   WebSphere for z/OS Connectivity Architectural Choices

3.3.1 EXCI pipes

A CICS TG provides a multi-threaded model for handling network connections, and for assigning threads for requests from and replies to Java client applications. Every thread is associated with an EXCI pipe. There is a limit of 100 pipes for every address space, such as a servant address space. A single CICS can support a maximum of 999 pipes. As a result, the 101st EXCI Allocate_Pipe call, made from a particular address space, will fail with an ECI_SYSTEM_ERROR. For complete details see the paragraph "EXCI pipe limitation" in *CICS Transaction Gateway z/OS Administration, Version 5.1*, SC43-6191-01.

> **Attention:** APAR PQ92943 for CICS TS V2 provides a configurable option to increase the EXCI pipe limit up to 250, using a new parameter in SYS1.PARMLIB.

The 100 pipe limit is usually sufficient to provide the required throughput, although the following points should be considered when designing a scalable CICS TG solution:

► The maximum number of JVM threads within a J2EE servant region is defined in the server workload profile. It has an upper maximum of either three times the number of CPUs or 40, depending on the setting of the application server workload profile, IOBOUND or LONGWAIT, respectively.

► For performance, once a call has been made to a CICS region from a given thread, the CICS TG will keep the pipe allocated to that particular CICS region for the lifetime of the thread, or until the CICS region terminates or closes IRC.

The J2CA connection pool managed by WebSphere Application Server is a set of local connection objects which map on the CICS TG JavaGateway connections. These connection objects do not map onto to the EXCI pipes allocated by the CICS TG. Instead EXCI pipes are allocated directly by the JVM threads within the WebSphere servant region.

An EXCI pipe shortage situation might only occur if multiple J2CA connection factories are used naming different CICS regions. This has the potential to cause pipes to become allocated to multiple CICS regions from a single thread. In this case, you should configure the J2EE servant region to have fewer threads, then use multiple servant regions to obtain the desired throughput. Alternatively, you can utilize the EXCI user exit DFHXCURM to cause all EXCI calls to go to the same local CICS routing region, before being forwarded onto the CICS application owning region (AOR), using CICSPlex Systems Manager (SM) or another routing technology.

Chapter 3. CICS connectivity options **55**

3.4 Local CICS connection

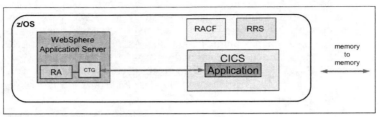

Figure 3-4   Local connection

In a local configuration, the CICS region is in the same z/OS LPAR as WebSphere. See Figure 3-4. A separate active CICS Transaction Gateway task is not required. The CICS TG is implemented inside of the WebSphere address space.

The CICS TG communicates with a CICS region in the same LPAR using a cross-memory implementation of ECI called EXCI. In this situation, the CICS TG local protocol can be used. This protocol directly invokes the underlying transport mechanism using the Java Native Interface (JNI) module libCTGJNI.so.

The CICS ECI resource adapter local mode configuration illustrated in Figure 3-4 was the only configuration option when CICS TG V5.0 was used with WebSphere for z/OS 4.01. It is also supported with WebSphere for z/OS V5 and CICS TG 5.1 and is the configuration that best exploits the advantages of the z/OS platform.

In local mode, there is no network between WebSphere and the CICS region. There are limited network security and delay concerns and the configuration is much simpler.

3.4.1 Local CICS connection: Attributes

Performance
- Best end-to-end performance
- Uses less memory than external CICS TG
- Takes advantage fo EXCI efficiencies

Availability
- Single z/OS image with two points of failure

Security
- RACF can be used for this configuration
- Thread Identity available for local resources via WebSphere

Transactionality
- Full two-phase commit

Scalability
- Vertical scaling with zSeries resources

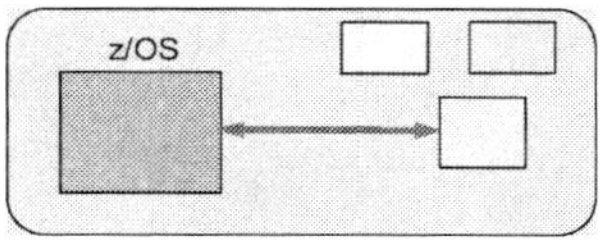

Figure 3-5   Local connection attributes

Performance

A local connection, as in Figure 3-5, provides better performance than a remote connection because no network overhead is involved in processing the request. Using a local CICS TG uses less CPU capacity than a remote connection CICS TG daemon because there is no separate CICS address space. The protocol is more efficient through the use of the cross-memory services.

You also eliminate the network latency from the WebSphere application to the CICS TG daemon. Performance also depends on the number of threads open, due to the amount of memory they use.

Within CICS there is a resource definition that defines the EXCI connection into CICS. The resource definition consists of a *connection* definition and a *sessions* definition. The CICS systems programmer should ensure that the number of sessions defined for the EXCI connection is greater than the number of EXCI pipes which are allocated by the WebSphere servant regions. The maximum number of sessions for an EXCI connection is 999.

Another factor indirectly limiting the number of threads and pipes through the EXCI to CICS is the number of Java threads in a servant region. This number cannot be set directly. The number of threads depends on the choice of Workload Profile.

Chapter 3. CICS connectivity options   **57**

Performance

Performance is affected by the number of pipes, threads and the number of servant regions. Because there are multiple limitations for the pipes, threads and number of servant regions, careful planning is required for a demanding workload. Also the workload heaviness, sheer volume, on the WebSphere and the CICS side influences how many servant regions are needed to optimize the throughput. It might be necessary to increase the number of servant regions, obtaining more threads, to achieve high workload levels.

Queuing work in the WebSphere servant regions uses excessive memory and drastically degrades the performance of the system. It is better to ensure that any queuing takes place in the HTTP Server in front of WebSphere.

Availability

On a single LPAR, a local connection has two points of failure:

► WebSphere Application Server
► the local CICS

There is no backup solution in this single LPAR case.

Transactional capabilities

This is a full-function, two-phase commit process with RRS coordinating the Resource Managers.

> **Note:** Use of a server isolation policy provides you the choice of running one transaction or multiple transactions per region. Executing more threads in an address space will provide better performance, but potentially at the cost of thread contention, which would be application-dependent. The thread value with the isolation policy is set in the ORB Services Advanced Setting.

Security

A local mode configuration is one that follows the traditional z/OS authentication model. That is, you authenticate at the entry point to z/OS. For a J2EE application it is normally in an HTTP Server or in WebSphere for z/OS. After authentication, your security identity, for example a Recourse Access Control Facility (RACF®) user ID, flows with you as you run work in different parts of the system.

If you have a J2EE application using J2CA to connect to CICS applications and you want to be able to identify the originator of the transactions running in CICS, however you authenticate in WebSphere, you need to associate a RACF user ID with the request to CICS.

For connections using container-managed authentication (res-auth=container) and in local mode with a local registry configured, WebSphere Thread Identity support passes the user ID associated with the current Java thread in WebSphere for z/OS to the CICS ECI resource adapter and then to CICS.

For a local mode connection, CICS uses EXCI, which is a protocol that allows non-CICS address spaces on z/OS to communicate with CICS. This protocol assumes that the z/OS address space has already been authenticated. Within the z/OS environment, this authentication has historically been based on user ID and password.

Once authentication has completed, it is not a good security to pass both the user ID and the password between address spaces because it increases the risk that the password might be exposed. That is why for an EXCI connection, CICS allows only two options on the ATTACHSEC property:

► ATTACHSEC=local

No user ID flows. CICS associates the LINK user ID if specified or the CICS region's default RACF user ID with any task initiated by a request from the EXCI connection

► ATTACHSEC=identify

The user ID flows with the request as the user named in the ECI request object or the user ID under which the ECI request runs.

Note: Authentication in WebSphere might not be based on user ID and password. Even if basic authentication or form-based login are used, the password is not available to be used for resource authentication of user ID and password at a later point. Therefore, for a container-managed application, the CICS ECI resource adapter will pass only the user ID to CICS and that user ID is used for authorization checking in CICS.

Normally CICS requires authentication. Because WebSphere and CICS are running on the same LPAR, there is a concept of trust. As a result, only a user ID flows from the WebSphere for z/OS address space to CICS. The password does not flow. Even if the application tries to pass a user ID and password, CICS will not authenticate. It only uses the flowed user ID when making authorization checks.

Between WebSphere for z/OS and CICS there are several SAF (RACF) checks made in the EXCI interface to control which address spaces and which users can connect to CICS. For this reason, local mode does not reduce your security. It increases security. After linking to CICS, the WebSphere application server passes an identity to CICS with each connection request.

Chapter 3. CICS connectivity options **59**

The CICS RA supports the following authentication methods:

- Container-managed (res-auth=container)

  The WebSphere container is responsible for passing security information to the CICS ECI resource adapter

- Application-managed (res-auth=application)

  The application must supply user ID and password.

Thread identity in WebSphere for z/OS applies only to container-managed connections. It allows the container to pass the security identity of the current Java thread to the J2CA connector and then to the CICS. The user ID passed is the RunAs identity of the EJB that calls the Connector. This could be:

- RunAs - Server, the application server's user ID
- RunAs - Caller, the identity of the caller of the EJB
- RunAs - Role, a user ID associated with a role

It is the absence of an association between the connection factory and a JAAS Authentication Alias that enables Thread Identity support and causes the identity on the current thread to be passed to the CICS ECI resource adapter. Therefore, you should not define a JAAS Authentication Alias unless you want to prevent user ID propagation and instead want to associate a fixed user ID (the JAAS Alias) with all requests to that CICS ECI connection factory.

If you want to use a JAAS Authentication Alias, and you want to authenticate the user ID and password coded on the alias, then you can tell the CICS ECI resource adapter to perform a user ID and password check by defining the WebSphere Environment Variable, AUTH_USERID_PASSWORD. Use the Administration Console for this task.

However, for a local mode connection, you will have authenticated the requester in WebSphere. Authenticating the JAAS Authentication Alias does not add any extra security to your configuration.

Scalability

The system can be vertically scaled by increasing CPU capacity (number, speed), memory, channels and other zSeries resources.

By configuring a Parallel Sysplex®, WebSphere for z/OS can be horizontally scaled across multiple machines and a cluster. Within an LPAR, WLM can start multiple servant regions.

3.5 Remote connection to CICS TG in same LPAR

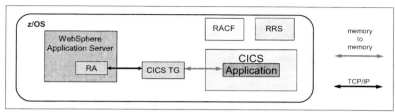

Figure 3-6 Remote connection in same LPAR

A separate CICS TG address space has been added. This introduces a network (TCP/IP) connection between WebSphere and the CICS TG running the same LPAR. Communication between the CICS TG address space and CICS uses EXCI. See Figure 3-6.

Even though both WebSphere and CICS run in the same z/OS LPAR, the external CICS TG requires an internal z/OS TCP/IP connection from the WebSphere address space. We lose all the advantages of the local pattern, even though all the software components run in the same LPAR.

However, there are some reasons why a user might want to configure their system this way. Consider a scenario where the user requires affinity to WebSphere and there are multiple CICS AORs to which the transaction can connect.

Another possible scenario is an application that requires separation by transaction types. In this example, imagine a transaction that is very high priority, fast and quick response time. An example is bank balance. There is a second transaction that is low priority, and long running. An example is a long report. In this case, we always want to make sure the first transaction gets serviced.

This can be achieved by configuring external CICS TGs to always have sufficient available pipes to service this transaction and a separate CICS TG for the lower priority transaction. The WebSphere application chooses the network address based on transaction type to direct the request. This approach of pooling of CICS TG pipes can be a very effective way of managing different classes of CICS transactions.

The programmer has to evaluate non-functional requirements to make an architectural decision. When evaluating local versus remote CICS TG connections, performance is only one consideration. All the attributes have to be reviewed.

3.5.1 Remote connection to CICS TG in same LPAR: Attributes

Performance
- Increase path length due to network connection
- Requests flow over TCP/IP
- Uses addtional address space

Security
- JAAS Authentication Alias

Scalability
- Vertical scaling with zSeries resources

Availability
- Single z/OS image with three points of failure

Transactionality
- One-phase commit support

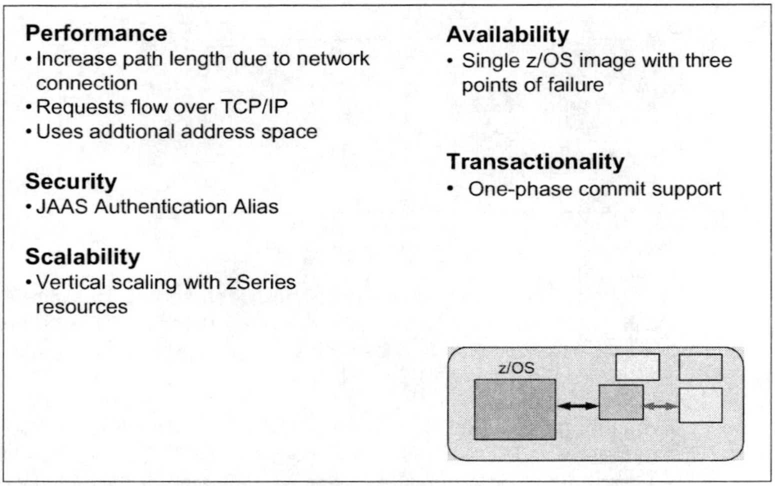

Figure 3-7   Remote connection in same LPAR - attributes

Performance

There are a couple of things worth mentioning about performance in Figure 3-7:

- ► Uses more memory due to additional address space
- ► Increases path length from WebSphere to CICS due network connection and use of TCP/IP stacks

Security

Thread identity is not passed over the TCP/IP connection so a JAAS authentication mechanism can be used.

On a remote mode connection, res-auth=application could be used and a user ID and password can sent to the CICS TG Daemon.

Availability

There are three points of failure:

- ► WebSphere
- ► CICS TG
- ► CICS in a single z/OS address space

However, this solution does offer pooling and the separation of pipes based on application and transaction processing requirements that are discussed in 3.5, "Remote connection to CICS TG in same LPAR" on page 61.

Transactional capabilities

When CICS TG is not executing inside the WebSphere address space, then it is only possible to have single-phase commit because the TCP/IP connection between WebSphere and CICS TG is based on ECI protocol. The ECI protocol that flows across a TCP/IP connection supports single-phase commit only.

Because WebSphere access to CICS on the same LPAR uses a remote connection, RRS manages their protected resources independently of each other. Two-phase commit can not be supported between WebSphere and CICS.

ECI is an IP protocol while EXCI was built to talk to RRS to exploit WebSphere CICS TG integration for two-phase commit.

Scalability

The system can be vertically scaled by increasing CPU capacity (number, speed), memory, channels and other zSeries resources.

Chapter 3. CICS connectivity options **63**

3.6 Remote CICS connection

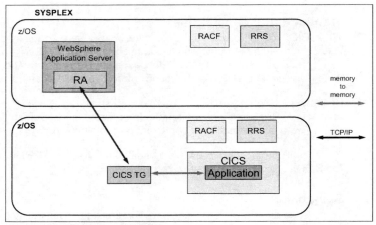

Figure 3-8   Remote connection

In a remote configuration, a CICS Transaction Gateway task must be active and listening for a request on the same LPAR as the CICS region on a different machine or LPAR from WebSphere. The CICS TG daemon is shown in Figure 3-8 connecting to a CICS system using the EXCI protocol.

New with WebSphere for z/OS V5 and CICS TG 5.01 for z/OS is the ability to have a remote connection to a CICS TG daemon, running on another z/OS LPAR. This solution implies that you must separate WebSphere and CICS with a TCP/IP network. You can adopt some kind of firewall between WebSphere and your business CICS systems.

3.6.1 Remote CICS connection: Attributes

Performance
- Introduces one more address space and a second LPAR
- Requests flow over TCP/IP across LPARs
- Uses addtional address space

Security
- JAAS Authentication Alias

Scalability
- Horizontal scaling with additional LPARs for WebSphere or CICS

Availability
- Three points of failure in two z/OS images
- Provides complete isolation between WebSphere and CICS

Transactionality
- Single-phase commit support

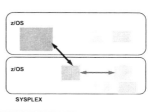

Figure 3-9   Remote connection attributes

Performance

A remote connection does not have the performance of a local connection because you have to pass through two TCP/IP stacks and a network to reach the CICS TG daemon. See the drawing in Figure 3-9. The daemon also includes some instruction path length, which you do not have in a local mode configuration.

Availability

This architecture introduces a second z/OS LPAR. This configuration does provide complete isolation between WebSphere and CICS. There are several reasons you might want this option. One is the CICS z/OS system might already exist, supporting users who do not use WebSphere.

When you implement a new WebSphere application, you bolt it in front of the CICS system and create a new entry point into CICS. However, from a total system view, there are more points of possible failure: WebSphere, CICS TG, CICS and two z/OS images.

In the WebSphere Application Server, you can have more than one servant region using the maximum number of connections they can open. See 3.4.1, "Local CICS connection: Attributes" on page 57. We can have a bottleneck because the CICS TG can create up to 100 connections. This is not a real problem because a high number of threads using memory degrades performance. A user would not implement so many threads.

Transactional capabilities

In this scenario, we are not able to exploit the two-phase commit transaction support provided by RRS. As a result, it lacks one of the main advantages of the local mode configuration. The link from WebSphere to the CICS TG daemon is a single-phase commit connection. Any global transaction context is not propagated from WebSphere into CICS. You can use the Last Participant Support built into WebSphere for z/OS V5.01. WebSphere ensures that CICS is the last participant in a global transaction as a single-phase commit capable resource and can participate in a global transaction.

Security

In the remote scenario, it is not possible to have Thread Identity. The Java Authentication and Authorization Service (JAAS) should be used.

The JAAS authentication alias is a way to specify a predefined user ID and password, which can be associated with requests to a particular connection factory. The JAAS authentication alias flows from the application client to CICS.

The CICS TG daemon can be configured to perform user ID password validation. To enable the CICS TG to authenticate each user ID and password flowed on an ECI request, the environment variable AUTH_USERID_PASSWORD must be set in the CICS TG environment variables. If user ID and password checking is not performed, it might be necessary to devise a way to establish a trust relationship between the application server and the Gateway daemon so that the application server can be trusted to flow only the user ID on the request through to CICS through the Gateway daemon. Solutions such as SSL client authentication can be used to establish such a trust relationship.

If the application authenticates using user ID and password, the application could use res-auth=application to pass the user ID and password to the CICS TG, which could be configured to authenticate.

Consideration

In the remote mode configuration you do not need to run CICS on the same LPAR as WebSphere. That offers complete separation of the WebSphere and CICS LPAR with no shared data or cross-memory communication. This might be a requirement of your security design.

This separation can also be achieved by running a pure CICS routing region in the WebSphere LPAR. That routing region need not share anything with any CICS in the CICS production LPAR and even be a different release of CICS.

3.7 Local CICS with increased availability

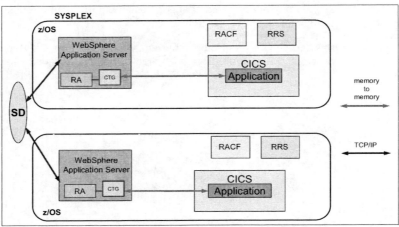

Figure 3-10 Local connection with increased availability

Building on the single system, local configuration model, Figure 3-10 adds a second z/OS Websphere Application Server WebSphere CICS LPAR. The addition of Sysplex Distributor (SD) allows for horizontal scaling the zSeries complex to increase performance and availability. This configuration provides enhanced availability and workload management over the single system configuration. z/OS Sysplex Distributor with WLM can provide traditional z/OS system workload management based on performance goals.

If the application must be Web-aware, state has to be managed in WebSphere or CICS. See *Workload Management for Web Access to CICS,* SG24-6118. This architecture also takes advantage of horizontal scaling to add computing resources. In summary, the Sysplex Distributor in this configuration provides two functions:

- Balancing of IP packets across multiple z/OS IP stacks using WLM
- Failover of the cluster IP address

One consideration that must be examined with this configuration is the possibility of a storm drain. This was discussed in "Architectural considerations" on page 1.

3.7.1 Local CICS with increased availability: Attributes

Performance
- Increase performance by adding multiple WebSphere+CICS LPARs
- Sysplex Distributor and WLM will balance workload across LPARs

Availability
- Fail-over support of cluster IP address provided by SD
- Non-disruptive quiesce of WebSphere CICS LPAR by SD redirecting IP traffic
- "Storm-Drain" possibility must be evaluated

Security
- Easiest method to handle security between WebSphere and CICS – trust z/OS address space
- Thread identity passed from WebSphere to CICS

Transactionality
- Complete two-phase commit is supported by RRS because CICS TG is in the WebSphere address space

Scalability
- Each WebSphere CICS LPAR can be independently vertically scaled (CPU, ...)
- Horizontal scaling possible by adding more LPARs and enlarging the WebSphere cluster

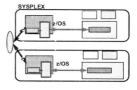

Figure 3-11   Local connection with increased availability attributes

Performance

This configuration has the performance of local connect for WebSphere CICS communications by using cross-memory services. Added performance improvements can be achieved by sysplex distributor balancing of IP packets across multiple z/OS IP stacks. Balancing is enabled by using a single cluster IP address which routes packets onto multiple nodes. See Figure 3-11.

The WebSphere servers must all be listening on the same port on the target nodes. Sysplex distributor also provides close integration with z/OS WLM policy agent and Service Level Agreements (SLA) in making the routing decisions.

Based on performance criteria, the arriving message is routed to the WebSphere CICS system that provides the best services. Performance can be improved by adding computing resources to the sysplex environment, known as horizontal scaling.

Availability

The addition of the second LPAR, accessed through sysplex distributor, will increase the availability by providing fail-over of the cluster IP address and re-routing of IP packets away from a inoperative node. The cluster IP address is actually a DVIPA and can be dynamically routed to another z/OS LPAR in the sysplex. This allows for failover of the cluster address.

Note that DVIPA take-back also allows for dynamic take-back of the address to the original adapter.

The cluster address can be instructed to no longer route further packets to a certain virtual IP address (VIPA). This allows work to be directed away from a WebSphere CICS system which is to be quiesced and onto another region on a different IP stack. The LPAR can be quiesced, without disrupting any of the inbound IP packets.

Nondisruptive movement of server applications can also occur when used in conjunction with a sysplex distributor. By utilizing the nondisruptive DVIPA capabilities, the impact of planned outages can be greatly reduced. What this means to workload management is that there is now a workload distribution and failover mechanism that is positioned at the entry to the WebSphere CICS system.

Unlike Domain Name System (DNS) connection optimization, this allows dynamic workload balancing without the overhead a DNS query, and allows for packets returning from the selected server to efficiently routed back through the distributing stack.

For more information on both Sysplex Distributor and dynamic Virtual IP Address (DVIPA), refer to the latest version of *TCP/IP in a Sysplex,* SG24-5235.

Since the CICS environment normally has its own workload balancing and failover, there is a potential problem of a failure of the CICS region that owns the EXCI connection to the WebSphere servants. By using the DFHXCURM exit, it is possible to provide failover for the EXCI connection between WebSphere servants and the target CICS system.

Security

This configuration has the same security considerations as discussed in section 3.4, "Local CICS connection" on page 56. The key point is the ability to flow the authenticated user ID from WebSphere to CICS Thread Identity support in WebSphere for z/OS.

Transactional capabilities

Like the Section 3.4, "Local CICS connection" on page 56, each system has complete two-phase commit supported by RRS.

If the WebSphere CICS application has to be Web-aware, then state information has to be handled by either WebSphere or CICS. The technique for CICS to handle state information is similar to that used by the CICS Web Services (CWS) sample state management utilities.

In addition, if you wish to balance workload, your Web request across multiple CICS regions, you will need to store any CICS state data in a place that is available to any CICS region, and ideally shareable across your sysplex. For more information please see *Workload Management for Web Access to CICS*, SG24-6118.

Scalability

The SD in front of the WebSphere CICS system provides horizontal scaling. Additional WebSphere CICS LPARs can be added to increase capacity and availability. SD with WLM will make routing decisions to satisfy Service Level Agreements.

> **Note:** Adding more parallel systems can increase the possibility of storm drain scenario. The loss of any CICS back-end will pull the incoming traffic to that system, causing the storm drain.

See Section 3.8, "Routing CICS local to remote" on page 72 for more information about avoiding the storm drain problem by using a CICS Routing region.

Chapter 3. CICS connectivity options   **71**

3.8 Routing CICS local to remote

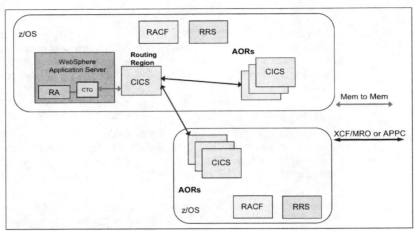

Figure 3-12   Local routing region

The architecture in Figure 3-12 builds on the benefits of WebSphere and CICS as local, but also satisfies the requirement to switch to an alternate z/OS CICS application-owning region (AOR) for availability.

This configuration introduces the concept of the CICS Routing Region. WebSphere has the requirement to connect to a CICS AOR in the same system image. However, in this configuration instead of going directly to the AOR, WebSphere attaches to a CICS Routing Region.

The CICS Routing Region makes the decision of which AOR to route the transaction. What is important here is it makes no difference where the AOR is located, it can be local or remote. This greatly increase availability because if the local AOR becomes unavailable then the transaction can be switched to alternate remote AOR by the CICS Routing Region.

Another major benefit of this configuration is its support for two-phase commit across the total system. The AORs do not have to be in the same system image as WebSphere. The AOR can be on a different LPAR in the sysplex or on a completely different system. If the CICS TG cannot be in the WebSphere address space, as discussed in Section 3.6, "Remote CICS connection" on page 64, then single-phase commit has to be implemented with CICS being the last participant. Integrating WebSphere to the back-end CICS system through a Routing Region is a best practice.

To enhance availability, CICSPlex SM can be used. It provides a single point of control from which all CICS systems can be managed, in a single system image manner. Multiple points of control can be established, eliminating any single point of failure in the management network, and providing appropriate span of control through SAF compliant security products.

Using CICSPlex SM in a router CICS region to balance requests to CICS AORs in another LPAR means that you separate the CICS production applications transaction from the WebSphere environment. To do this, use two types of CICS regions:

1. The *CICS Listener* runs in the same LPAR as WebSphere and only acts as a router to the actual CICS region.

2. The *CICS AOR* runs on a separate LPAR. This CICS region runs the CICS transaction.

Traditionally, a CICSPlex SM environment consisted of one or more terminal-owning regions (TORs) connected to a group of application-owning regions (AORs). This is known as a *hub model*, and the design assumes that the workload originates in the TOR and is then routed to run in one of the AORs. Thus, in a hub model the TOR acts as router for transactions and the AORs execute the transactions.

Since the advent of CICS Web-enablement, the term TOR is no longer always appropriate, because work is not initiated from a traditional 3270 CICS terminal but from a Web browser, which can be connected to CICS in a variety of ways. Requests can arrive through the CICS TCP/IP listener, an EXCI connection, or a a traditional LU6.2 connection. We therefore refer to a CICS region which is participating in receiving such Web requests as a *listener region*.

Starting with CICS TS V1.3, it is possible to dynamically route a request received by the listener region to one of the multiple cloned AORs. This functionality is called *dynamic program link* (DPL). In this architecture, there is only one CICS listener in each LPAR, and it might be a single point of failure. Because this CICS listener only acts as a router to the actual CICS AOR, and no application logic is located there, it is very unlikely to fail. If it does, ARM can be used to restart the CICS listener very quickly.

If this is not acceptable in your environment, multiple listeners can be implemented using the EXCI user-replaceable module DFHXCURM. A detailed description to set up such a high availability environment can be found in *Workload Management for Web Access to CICS,* SG24-6118.

Chapter 3. CICS connectivity options **73**

3.8.1 Routing CICS local to remote: Attributes

Performance
- WebSphere access to local CICS AOR for best performance
- CICS routing program to multiple AORs with low system overhead
- CICS traditional performance management

Availability
- Remote CICS can be accessed if local CICS is unavailable
- CICSPlex/SM can provide enhanced routing and availability capabilities
- ARM can start CICS listener very quickly

Security
- Thread identity passed from WebSphere container to routing region
- Once CICS is called, CICS security is used

Transactionality
- If CICS TG is local to WebSphere then full two-phase commit across all systems
- If CICS TG in separate address space from WebSphere then single-phase commit with CICS as Last Participant

Scalability
- Local WebSphere CICS can be vertically scaled (CPU, memory, channels, ...)
- Remote CICS AOR can be vertically or horizontally scaled (more systems added)

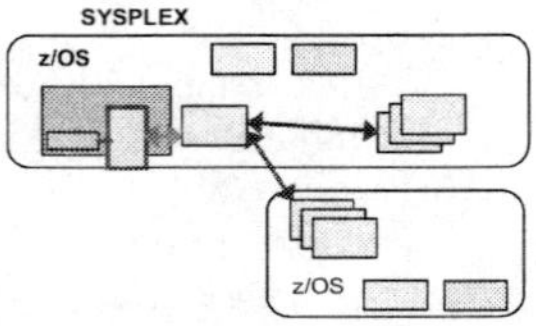

Figure 3-13 Local routing region attributes

Performance

This configuration has all the performance benefits of local WebSphere CICS configuration with a small overhead for the routing region. See Figure 3-13. The performance of the CICS portion of the system is well understood and only the performance of WebSphere needs to be included in the total performance consideration. Traditional CICS performance management techniques can be employed.

The main advantage of this configuration is that if more CICS computing resources are required in addition to the local CICS resources, additional AORs can be created on other LPARs on the sysplex, or a separate z/OS system, to meet performance goals. If WebSphere requires more resources, then CICS AORs can even be moved off the z/OS image leaving only the routing region without lost of the two-phase commit capability.

Availability

This configuration provides back-end CICS AOR availability with the addition of the CICS routing region. If the local CICS AOR becomes unavailable, then the CICS routing region can switch the transaction to a remote AOR. CICSPlex SM provides a single point of control for all CICS regions.

WebSphere for z/OS Connectivity Architectural Choices

It also can dynamically route workload for balancing or workload separation. If the CICS listener should become unavailable, ARM can be used to restart it very quickly. For more information, refer to *Workload Management for Web Access to CICS,* SG24-6118.

Security

This configuration uses the security model presented in section 3.4, "Local CICS connection" on page 56. When using a local mode connection, you do not normally need to be concerned about establishing trust for requests from WebSphere for z/OS. This avoids the need for SSL or a firewall configuration between WebSphere and CICS. Therefore, your configuration activities are much simpler. There are fewer points of failure. However, you should still take steps to protect access to your CICS server. MRO bind security can be used to establish a trust relationship between the application server and CICS servers. It is implemented using DFHAPPL profiles in the RACF FACILITY class that control logon to DFHIRP.

You can have separation of the WebSphere and business CICS environments using a local mode connection to a CICS routing region in the same LPAR as WebSphere. Then the CICS routing region uses CICS InterSystem Communication facilities to route requests to the business CICS systems in the other LPAR using LU6.2.

If your company security policy insists on some kind of firewall between WebSphere and your CICS systems, that implies that you must separate WebSphere and CICS with a TCP/IP network. However, the RACF controls on the EXCI connection between WebSphere and the router CICS, plus the switch of communication protocol to LU6.2 will provide much better security than using a TCP/IP network and a firewall. Local mode does not reduce your security, it increases it.

If the CICS TG is configured in its own address space, then thread identity can not be used. See section 3.5, "Remote connection to CICS TG in same LPAR" on page 61. The security consideration for this configuration is the same as discussed in section 3.5.1, "Remote connection to CICS TG in same LPAR: Attributes" on page 62.

Transactional capabilities

This configuration provides full two-phase commit across WebSphere and CICS if the CICS TG is implemented local to WebSphere. This solution attractive because the two-phase commit is not limited to the local z/OS image or even sysplex. The CICS AOR can be on any z/OS system. CICS with the use of the routing region will coordinate the commit for all CICS resources.

Chapter 3. CICS connectivity options   **75**

If the CICS TG is implemented in its own address space as in section 3.5.1, "Remote connection to CICS TG in same LPAR: Attributes" on page 62, then WebSphere can only support single-phase commit and CICS has to be the last participant.

Scalability

The local WebSphere CICS system can be vertically scaled just as described in section 3.4, "Local CICS connection" on page 56. The system can be scaled by increasing CPU capacity (number, speed), memory, channels and other zSeries resources.

Another way to increase system capacity of WebSphere is to move CICS to other LPARs and let CICS routing region or CICSPlex SM manage the workload. CICS resources can be increased by use of horizontal scaling technique. LPARs for AORs can be added for more z/OS computing resources.

3.9 Remote CICS with availability

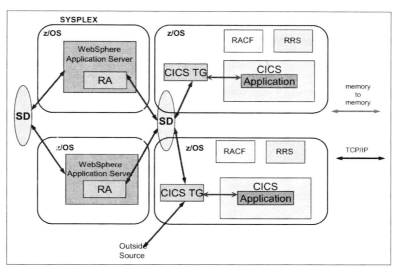

Figure 3-14   Remote connection with availability

Figure 3-14 and Figure 3-16 on page 81 compare two availability system architectures. They both are built on system architecture principles that were described earlier in this book. The key feature they have in common is both separate WebSphere from CICS application AORs. This allows isolation of major system components to increase performance management, availability and scalability.

The configuration implemented above is the CICS remote connectivity pattern. You use a remote connection to a CICS TG when you want to run your WebSphere for z/OS server in an LPAR which is totally separated from the LPAR running your CICS system. You might want to do this to avoid any data-sharing or XCF communications between the WebSphere and CICS LPARs. Your security manager might insist on this separation as part of the security design.

Another reason for selecting this configuration could be migration. You are driven here mainly to satisfy the requirement to support the existing infrastructure. To understand this, imagine only the right side of the illustration above is in production. The enterprise supports multiple CICS regions. A user accesses the CICS system through the existing remote CICS TG. Multiple CICS TGs may be balanced through a Sysplex Distributor. The CICS TG may be attached to CICS Routing Region.

Chapter 3. CICS connectivity options   **77**

The key point is when the decision is made to add the WebSphere infrastructure, the decision is to bolt the WebSphere in front of CICS to maintain as much as possible of the existing infrastructure. To increase capacity and availability of WebSphere, LPARs can be added using Sysplex Distributor and WLM.

This configuration builds on the remote connection. Sysplex Distributor has been configured to service both WebSphere and CICS Transaction Gateways. In this configuration, WebSphere is connected to CICS Transaction Gateway (CICS TG) using TCP/IP connections. As discussed in the remote connection scenario, above, TCP/IP connections are required for inter-LPAR connections.

The benefits of a SD that were provided to WebSphere are now also provided to establish the connections from WebSphere to CICS TG. Sysplex Distributor with WLM performance data establishes a connection to CICS TG that is best suited to service a connection request. However, the connection will stay static for the life of the connection, regardless of performance.

If any WebSphere applications become inoperative, then Sysplex Distributor routes the traffic to the alternate system. If any CICS TG should become inactive, then Sysplex Distributor establishes a new connection to an alternative CICS TG based on WLM performance information. This connection stays intact until it is terminated.

3.9.1 Remote CICS with availability: Attributes

Performance
- Not as good as local
- Sysplex Distributor(SD) and WLM will balance workload across WebSphere LPARs
- Single Cluster IP address

Availability
- No single point of failure
- Availability improved with Sysplex Distributor

Security
- Security the same as remote connection case

Transactional capabilities
- Single-phase commit with CICS as Last Participant
- If the application must handle affinity then WebSphere or CICS must handle since SD does not handle affinity
- If communication goes down during a transaction, recovery may be routed to a different CICS TG that does not know about transactional state

Scalability
- Vertical scaling of each LPAR by increasing resources
- Horizontal scaling by adding LPARs and resources to WebSphere or CICS regions
- Sysplex Distributor and WLM can workload balance WebSphere LPARs to meet performance goals

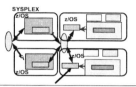

Figure 3-15   Remote connection attributes

Performance

See Figure 3-15. The main performance attributes of this configuration have been discussed previously. The key disadvantage is using a TCP/IP connection is not as efficient as a local connection. The advantages are the complete isolation of WebSphere and CICS components, which can allow for the horizontal scaling of computing resources where needed.

This configuration uses Sysplex Distributor with WLM to manage the workload in front of WebSphere. If you choose this configuration due to migration considerations, then the performance of the CICS portion of the infrastructure is known. To establish the Service Level Agreement (SLA) of the total system, the WebSphere portion of the performance budget can be measured and scaled to meet the performance goals.

Availability

One of the positive features of this configuration is that it can be designed for no single points of failure. In the migration case, the availability CICS portion of this system is known. By placing WebSphere in its own LPARs, system component failures can be isolated. Multiple WebSphere regions can be added and managed by Sysplex Distributor and WLM to increase availability and to meet availability goals.

Security

The security considerations of this configuration are the same as discussed in the section 3.6, "Remote CICS connection" on page 64. The configuration offers complete isolation between CICS and WebSphere.

Of particular note, if this is a migration consideration, then you must review and understand your current security implementation and requirements. This establishes your baseline of security requirements. Then you must review if the current security is adequate for an e-business infrastructure, or if additional security must be added.

After this has been established, modifications to the CICS systems can be made to meet the new security requirements and WebSphere security can implemented using some of the techniques described above and in *WebSphere Application Server for z/OS Version 5 and J2EE Security Handbook*, SG24-6086.

Transactional capabilities

The consideration for transactional capabilities are the same as discussed in the section 3.6, "Remote CICS connection" on page 64. Only single-phase commit is supported between WebSphere and CICS.

If the transaction has to maintain state to be Web-aware then WebSphere and CICS state maintenance techniques have to be employed, see *Workload Management for Web Access to CICS*, SG24-6118.

Sysplex Distributor does not handle affinity. In case of a communication error, the roll-back transaction might go to another CICS TG that does not know about the transactional state.

Scalability

This and the following configurations offer the best solution for scaling. Each WebSphere and CICS LPAR can be vertically scaled to add computing resources. However, this configuration is capable of exploiting horizontal scaling using Sysplex Distributor and WLM. New WebSphere and CICS LPARs can be added to the sysplex to increase capacity and availability as needed to meet the SLA performance goals. See techniques for scaling as described earlier.

3.10 Remote with availability using CICS routing

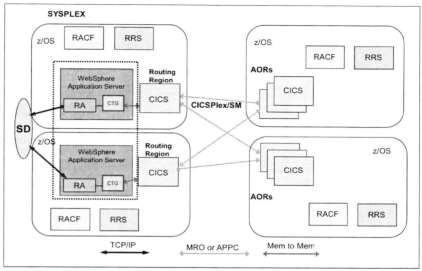

Figure 3-16   High availability remote connection with routing regions

The solution in Figure 3-16 is considered best practice. The architecture builds on the previous two configurations. The major difference between this configuration and the previous one is the CICS TG and the a CICS Routing Region is co-located in the WebSphere LPAR. This provides several benefits:

- The application in WebSphere can connect to the CICS TG and CICS through the local connect using MRO. This is a considerable performance enhancement over the remote CICS TG option.

- It supports two-phase commit between WebSphere and CICS. WebSphere can take advantage of horizontal scaling using Sysplex Distributor and WLM to increase capacity for better performance and availability.

- If migration or coexistence with an existing environment is required, then the CICS LPARs will require little, if any, modification because the CICS complex can use its existing routing structure for connectivity.

- WebSphere along with the local CICS TG and CICS Routing Region only have to be added, or bolted on, to the front of the CICS system using CICSPlex SM. It is the CICSPlex SM with the routing regions that provide the connectivity and availability. This configuration also provides isolation from the CICS business AORs in the back-end region.

One consideration that must be reviewed with this configuration is the possibility of a storm drain. If the connection from WebSphere to the CICS Routing Region or the Routing Region itself is lost, then that WebSphere server will appear to have better performance and the Sysplex Distributor and WLM will direct work towards it. There are ways to reduce this concern discussed in the section 3.8, "Routing CICS local to remote" on page 72.

3.10.1 Remote availability with CICS routing: Attributes

Performance
- WebSphere can use SD and WLM to meet LPAR performance goals
- Implements CICS best practice solution for performance management
- Takes advantage of WebSphere access to local CICS routing region for performance
- Uses CICS routing program to access multiple AORs with low system overhead

Availability
- Provides greatest amount of availability due to no single point of failure
- CICSPlex SM can provide enhanced routing and availability capabilities

Security
- Same security considerations as discussed in "Routing CICS local to remote"

Transactional capabilities
- If CICS TG is local to WebSphere then full two-phase commit across all systems

Scalability
- Local WebSphere or CICS can be vertically scaled (CPU, memory, channels, ...)

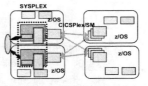

Figure 3-17   High availability remote connection with routing region

Performance

This configuration in Figure 3-17 takes advantage of the performance enhancements offered by Sysplex Distributor and WLM for WebSphere, and is identical to the last configuration. The major difference between this configuration and the last is the use of the local CICS TG to WebSphere and the use of CICS Routing Region in the LPAR.

This local connection to the routing region provides better performance then the remote connection and supports two-phase commits. The second advantage is the routing region (CICSPlex SM) provides true dynamic routing to the AOR providing better performance. Multiregion operation (MRO) connectivity between LPARs generally has better performance than TCP/IP.

The previous configuration using Sysplex Distributor and DVIPA only provided dynamic connection to the AOR with the best performance at the time of connection. After the connection was established, the routing was static through the life of the connection regardless of the performance of the CICS AORs. Like the last configuration, the performance of the CICS portion of this configuration is well understood. To establish the SLA for the total system, WebSphere portion can be scaled to meet the performance goals. The total system performance can be managed using a combination of Sysplex Distributor and WLM for WebSphere and CICSPlex SM for the CICS portion of the system.

Availability

CICSPlex SM is the best practice for connecting WebSphere to CICS. This architecture builds on Switch local to remote architecture. That architecture provides CICS application availability through CICS dynamic routing. The WebSphere CICS system availability is increased by adding Sysplex Distributor with WLM in front of WebSphere. This eliminates WebSphere from being a single point of failure by allowing Sysplex Distributor to route traffic to the alternate, available Websphere Application Server.

The use of one CICS TG and CICS Routing Region could possibly become a single point of failure and a possible storm drain. To solve this problem, a second CICS TG and CICS Routing Region should be created. Then ARM can be used to restart the CICS listener very quickly.

If this is not acceptable in your environment, multiple listeners can be implemented using the EXCI user-replaceable module DFHXCURM. DFHXCURM provides for simple fail-over and round-robin workload balancing by providing a means to capture retryable errors and modify the destination APPLID specified in the EXCI call.

Security

There are security advantages to using a CICS router. If you use a CICS TG, you have no possibility to customize security in the CICS TG environment. It is pretty much a black box. But when you use a CICS router, you have a lot more possibilities. For example, CICSPlex SM allows you to add your own code to the routing decision in EYU9WRAM.

Transactional capabilities

This architecture provides full two-phase commit across WebSphere and CICS environments if the CICS TG is implemented local to WebSphere with CICS routing region in the same LPAR. This solution is attractive because two-phase commit is not limited to the local z/OS image or even sysplex. The CICS AOR can be on any z/OS system. CICS with the use of the routing region will coordinate the commit for all CICS resources.

Chapter 3. CICS connectivity options   **83**

If CICS TG is implemented in its own address space as in section 3.5, "Remote connection to CICS TG in same LPAR" on page 61, then WebSphere can only support single-phase commit with CICS and CICS has to be the Last Participant.

Scalability

The increase in capacity of the WebSphere CICS system over Switch local to remote is accomplished by adding WebSphere servers with Sysplex Distributor and WLM. Sysplex Distributor with WLM will route the transactions to the WebSphere server best able to handle the work. If a WebSphere server becomes unavailable, then the following transactions will be routed to the alternate WebSphere server.

Every component in this architecture can be vertically scaled within the limits of the zSeries hardware. The local WebSphere CICS routing region can be vertically scaled just as described in the section 3.4, "Local CICS connection" on page 56. The system can be scaled by increasing CPU capacity (number, speed), memory, channels and other zSeries resources.

WebSphere and the CICS resources can be increased by use of horizontal scaling techniques. LPARs for Websphere can be created and Sysplex Distributor will forward transactions to the WebSphere LPAR that can meet the performance goals. AORs can be allocated to add more z/OS computing resources and CICSPlex SM will dynamically route transaction based on performance and availability.

3.11 Accessing CICS using RMI/IIOP

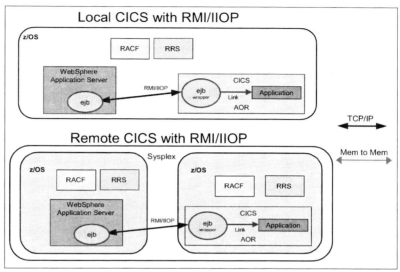

Figure 3-18   IIOP access

The previous sections have been devoted to the different architectural approaches of connecting WebSphere to CICS using the CICS Transaction Gateway. This CICS TG approach is the most widely-used and clients have used it before the introduction of Java Web systems.

However, as developers create new applications, there is a requirement that these new functions be able to be deployed anywhere. Java with Enterprise JavaBean support in CICS can provide this function.

A significant benefit of the introduction of support for Enterprise JavaBeans (EJB) into CICS is that it enables a whole new set of software development tools and practices with which to write software for the CICS environment.

One point you might have noticed reading previous sections and the other chapters of this book is the transaction is always initiated from the WebSphere server. That is because the focus of this book is connecting WebSphere to EIS, CICS in this case, and it is WebSphere that initiates the transaction.

CICS TS provides an environment for enterprise applications written in Java with an architecture that ensures that Java applications have a high degree of isolation from each other. Further, CICS has enhanced Java execution by improving behavior under stress, reducing storage and start-up requirements for a JVM.

CICS TS provides support for Enterprise JavaBeans, which enables clients such as servlets, session beans, and Java applications to invoke session beans running within the CICS EJB server. One of the components that make up the CICS EJB Server is the EJB container that creates and manages enterprise bean instances at run time, and isolates the enterprise beans from direct client access. The EJB container supports a number of implicit services, including security, transaction management, and persistence. These services are required by each enterprise bean running in the container.

Java application programs in CICS run under the control of CICS in a JVM that is initialized by CICS and runs within the CICS address space. Communication between EJBs is over RMI/IIOP:

► RMI

  Remote Method Invocation (RMI) is the Java language native mechanism for performing simple, powerful networking. RMI allows you to write distributed objects in Java, enabling objects to communicate in memory, across Java Virtual Machines, and across physical devices. RMI allows you to invoke methods on remote objects. You can build your network code as full objects. This yields the benefits of object-oriented programming, such as inheritance, encapsulation, and polymorphism.

► IIOP

  Internet InterORB Protocol is a communication technology used by CICS and provides a suitable opportunity for those considering Java and distributed object support as their future direction. You can chose either Java RMI between enterprise beans or CORBA client support.

Figure 3-18 on page 85 illustrates WebSphere connection to CICS address space. Notice in this picture there is no need for a CICS TG. Communication is accomplished by EJB method calls in WebSphere that resolve to a method on an EJB inside the CICS container. EJB communications is accomplished by RMI over IIOP. This protocol flows over a TCP/IP connection. It makes no difference if WebSphere and CICS are in the same z/OS LPAR or the are in different LPARs. The only difference is when they are in the same LPAR, the network is internal to z/OS. Figure 3-18 on page 85 shows both of these cases.

In this architecture a request comes into WebSphere EJB, the EJB makes a method call on an EJB in CICS known as a wrapper. The wrapper EJB is a thin EJB and its function is to link to a traditional CICS program. That EJB then exposes the CICS applications to Java clients capable of making RMI/IIOP calls. The EJB in CICS does a link to a CICS program communicating with it through the program's COMMAREA. The results of the link to the CICS program a returned to the CICS EJB and back to WebSphere.

3.11.1 Accessing CICS using RMI over IIOP: Attributes

Performance
- Overhead of CICS EJB wrapper
- Overhead of RMI over IIOP over TCP/IP

Availability
- Same considerations as local connection attributes
- EJB component availability has to be considered against CICS TG availability

Security
- Consideration are similar to remote mode J2CA connection

Transactionality
- Full J2EE transactionality between EJBs in WebSphere and CICS
- Full two-phase commit between WebSphere and CICS

Scalability
- If on one LPAR then LPAR can be vertically scaled
- If multiple LPARs then any component of the system can be horizontally scaled

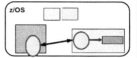

Figure 3-19 IIOP access attributes

Performance

The WebSphere connecting to CICS using RMI over IIOP does not require the CICS Resource Adapter to be installed (local mode) or a CICS Transaction Gateway daemon (remote mode). This reduction in path length comes at an expense that must be carefully considered. RMI over IIOP must use a TCP/IP network connection. See Figure 3-19.

This solution has the same performance draw-backs as the remote connect using CICS TG. As discussed in "Remote connection attributes," 3.6.1 on page 65, remote network connections do not have the performance of a local connection using EXCI.

There is also the added overhead of the RMI over IIOP protocol. This is even a larger performance hit than the CICS TG network connection.

Another performance consideration is the EJB, Java processing in the CICS container. This is an additional code path that is not in the CICS TG solution. These performance concerns have to be weighed against the new Java functionality.

The high level of abstraction required for Java, as an object-oriented language, involves increased layering and more dynamic run time binding as a necessary part of the run time environment. This incurs added costs at run time, but lots of efforts have been done to increase performance.

Availability

The availability is similar to Local and Remote CICS connection discussed above with CICS TG.

Security

Using RMI/IIOP to invoke an EJB in CICS currently has inferior function to a local mode J2CA connector. With J2CA in WebSphere for z/OS the Thread Identity support allows you to flow the identity of the current Java thread through to CICS and there is no network security to worry about. This is a strong requirement of most CICS customers because their audit trails, and, sometimes, CICS application functionality depends on having a user ID that is unique to a person.

If you decide to use IIOP rather than J2CA, then the considerations are similar to those of using a remote mode J2CA connection in that you will need to consider network security, firewalls and SSL, because you are passing user IDs over a TCP/IP network.

Individual enterprise beans do not need to authenticate users or check authorization levels explicitly. The EJB container can automatically perform all security checking on behalf of the enterprise bean. EJB security involves the following aspects:

- ▶ Encrypting the information flow (SSL support)
- ▶ Identifying the user (authentication)
- ▶ Controlling what the user can do (authorization)
- ▶ Controlling methods permissions (EJB roles)

SSL support

Accessing EJBs requires the use of the IIOP protocol. In order to protect the data over an insecure network, the Secure Sockets Layer (SSL) protocol can be used, providing both confidentiality and data integrity. Applets or Java applications may require the use of SSL. But a servlet or an enterprise bean running in WebSphere may not need SSL security. Both CICS and WebSphere are likely to be in your private network.

Authentication

Authentication is the technique used to identify the client user ID. In Java terms it is known as a Principal. In CICS terms, it means a user ID. Since CICS

88   WebSphere for z/OS Connectivity Architectural Choices

authorization is based on a user ID, we must derive one from the IIOP request. This user ID can be provided to CICS by:

- ► SSL client certificate

  In client authentication, the secret that authenticates the client is the client's private key, which is retained inside the client's workstation. During the SSL handshake, the certificate is authenticated and passed to RACF to determine if a user ID is associated with the certificate.

- ► Security user-replaceable module

  If no SSL client certificate is provided, you can assign a user ID by coding a user-replaceable module (URM). The URM should return a pointer to an 8-byte character field in its COMMAREA, and CICS will associate that user ID with the server transaction.

- ► Asserted identity authentication

  Asserted identity authentication can be used when an IIOP client communicates with the target server (CICS TS V2.3) through an intermediate server (in this case, WebSphere Application Server for z/OS), and both servers use the same security manager. It works as follows:

  - The application server's identity is authenticated by the target server using SSL client certificate authentication.

  - Through the security manager, the CICS region verifies that the application server can be trusted to authenticate its clients.

  - When the application server receives a request, it authenticates the client using whatever authentication protocol is appropriate. If the client is successfully authenticated, the application server passes the request to CICS.

  - Because CICS trusts the application server to authenticate the client, it makes no further checks of the client's authenticity before processing the client's request.

Authorization

Access control is concerned with checking if a user is authorized to access a particular method in a bean, and what this user can do inside the method. EJB permits two levels of access control.

EJB roles

Access to enterprise bean methods is based on the concept of security roles. A security role represents a user of an application in terms of the permissions that the user must have to successfully use the application.

The security roles for an application are defined by the application assembler, and are specified in the bean's deployment descriptor.

The mapping of deployed security roles to individual users or groups is done in the RACF classes EJBROLE and GEJBROLE.

Transactional capabilities

When a WebSphere EJB calls a CICS EJB, there is full J2EE transactional capability. There is full two-phase commit regardless if CICS is in the same LPAR or a different LPAR. This is an advantage that connection from WebSphere to CICS with RMI/IIOP has over remote connection with CICS TG. That solution only supports single-phase commit.

Scalability

If WebSphere and CICS are implemented on the same LPAR, then the only solution is vertical scaling. If WebSphere and CICS are on different LPARs, then each LPAR can be vertically and horizontally scaled

3.12 CICS RMI over IIOP with availability

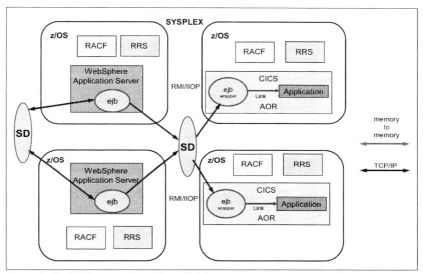

Figure 3-20   IIOP connection with availability

In Figure 3-20, Sysplex Distributor has been configured to service both WebSphere and CICS LPARs. In this configuration, WebSphere is connected to CICS using RMI/IIOP connections. CICS has IIOP listeners. Sysplex Distributor supports these IIOP listeners. If any WebSphere becomes inactive, then Sysplex Distributor routes the traffic to the alternate system. If any CICS becomes inactive then Sysplex Distributor directs the transaction to an alternative CICS listener based on WLM performance information.

3.12.1 CICS RMI/IIOP with availability: Attributes

Performance
- Increased performance by adding multiple WebSphere and CICS LPARs
- Sysplex Distributor and WLM will balance workload across WebSphere LPARs
- Multiple AORs with IIOP listener

Availability
- No single point of failure
- Availability improved with Sysplex Distributor

Security
- Security the same as remote connection case

Transactionality
- Full EJB transactionality with two-phase commit

Scalability
- Vertical scaling of each LPAR by increasing resources
- Horizontal scaling by adding LPARs and resources to WebSphere or CICS regions
- Sysplex Distributor and WLM can balance WebSphere LPARs to meet performance goals

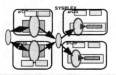

Figure 3-21 High availability IIOP connection attributes

Performance
In most of the discussion about performance in 3.9.1, "Remote CICS with availability: Attributes" on page 79, an EJB in CICS uses a single home interface that is published to the Java naming and directory interface (JNDI) server. Through the normal IP workload distribution mechanisms of sysplex distributor and port sharing, the RMI connection resolves to a specific instance of the CICS IIOP listener. This creates a highly available WebSphere CICS system. See Figure 3-21.

Availability, security and scalability
This is the same discussion as section "3.9.1, "Remote CICS with availability: Attributes" on page 79.

Transactional capabilities
There is full two-phase commit between WebSphere and CICS. WebSphere appears as an equal transaction manager to CICS. What this means is there is full transactional capability between all resources, EJBs and CICS-linked programs.

3.13 SOAP connection

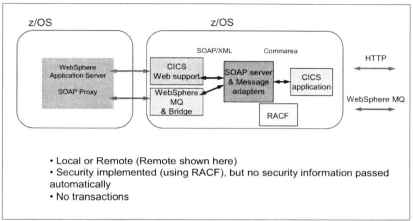

Figure 3-22   SOAP connection to CICS

In Figure 3-22, the Simple Object Access Protocol (SOAP) connection to CICS is a bidirectional communication option between WebSphere and CICS. A SOAP client in WebSphere can call the SOAP server in CICS and execute a CICS transaction. A CICS transaction can call a service in WebSphere using SOAP processing.

The message transport is either HTTP or WebSphere MQ over TCP/IP.

The CICS Web Support or WebSphere MQ gets the SOAP Extensible Markup Language (XML) message and passes it on to the SOAP server within CICS. A pipeline is established and assigned to the call. The pipeline is a series of processing that is done in order to transform the SOAP XML message into a traditional COMMAREA. The reverse is also true. At the end of the pipeline, the CICS transaction is called with a Distributed Program Link to execute the business logic. When it is done, the adapters transform and package the reply into a proper SOAP XML format and the transport handlers send it back to WebSphere.

This solution implements the service-oriented architecture (SOA) principle, but the attributes of the solution are not yet as good as the other choices, such as CICS TG.

3.13.1 SOAP connection: Attributes

Performance
- Slower than local because of network and SOAP/XML transformations

Availability
- Multiple Web Support listeners can be started, sharing ports.
- Multiple pipelines are established
- Traditional CICS availability with DPL

Security
- CICS uses RACF to check authentication; the SOAP components need authentication
- No userid/password is passed automatically from WebSphere

Transactional capabilities
- No

Scalability
- Multiple HTTP or WebSphere MQ listeners
- Multiple SOAP servers, multiple SOAP clients in WebSphere cluster
- Traditional CICS scalability with DPL

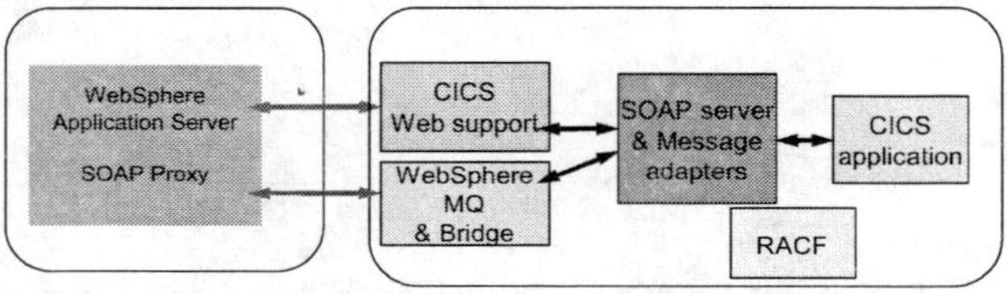

Figure 3-23   SOAP connection: Attributes

Performance

The performance is worse because of the network layers and the transformations. See Figure 3-23.

Availability

Availability can be increased by establishing multiple Web Support listeners and using port-sharing or sysplex distributor to balance requests. In case of WebSPhere MQ as transport, shared queues can be established. Multiple pipelines are built for each call and the Distributed Program Link can call transactions in multiple Application Owning Regions.

Security

Security is used by CICS calling RACF and each component should run under a valid RACF user ID, otherwise it fails. There are ways to change user IDs in this solution, but no security information is passed from WebSphere to the CICS SOAP server. SOAP headers can be processed on the WebSphere and CICS side to pass security information but no automatic processing occurs.

94   WebSphere for z/OS Connectivity Architectural Choices

Transactional capabilities

There is no transactional connection between WebSphere and CICS. The transactional context is not propagated from WebSphere. It is similar to sync-on-return processing. When the CICS transaction ends, commit occurs.

The solution can be scaled up by using multiple WebSphere servers in a cluster, multiple HTTP listeners, multiple SOAP servers, multiple pipelines and multiple CICS Application Owning Regions.

96   WebSphere for z/OS Connectivity Architectural Choices

4

IMS connectivity options

This chapter provides topology options connecting WebSphere Application Server on z/OS to IMS using a connector address space.

We describe basic scenarios used to attach IMS as the back-end system and explore the architectural behavior of each topology option. In either a local or remote configuration, IMS is accessed from the Websphere Application Server for z/OS through the IMS Connect task.

This chapter explains the following components:

- ► Information Management System (IMS) Resource Adapter (IMS Connector for Java), now called IMS V9 Integrated IMS Connector for Java function

- ► IMS Connect, now called IMS V9 Integrated IMS Connect function

- ► JDBC access through IMS Java classes

Note: We mention JDBC as another means to access IMS from Websphere Application Server for z/OS, although it is not explicitly displayed in the architectural diagram scenarios.

© Copyright IBM Corp. 2004. All rights reserved. **97**

4.1 Interface components: Resource adapter

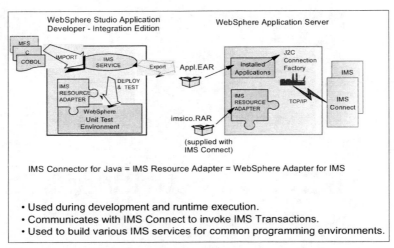

Figure 4-1   The IMS Resource Adapter

You can develop a Java application using the IBM WebSphere Studio Application Developer Integration Edition and the IMS Resource Adapter. WebSphere Studio Application Developer Integration Edition uses the IMS Resource Adapter to access IMS transactions running on a host IMS system.

The IMS Resource Adapter is used both during development and at run time. The WebSphere Studio Application Developer Integration Edition is a service-based development environment and the IMS resource adapter is one of the service providers included, it contains a collection of Java classes.

Here is a brief overview of how it works:

1. When a Java application is invoked, it presents a transaction request to IMS through the IMS Connect product. If IMS Connect resides on a different LPAR than the IMS Resource Adapter, the IMS resource adapter and IMS Connect use TCP/IP to communicate.

2. IMS Connect sends the transaction request to IMS OTMA using XCF (Cross-system Coupling Facility) and the transaction executes in IMS. The response is returned to the Java application using the same path.

You can use the IMS Resource Adapter to build an IMS connection from COBOL, C, or MFS source files. There are two types of IMS J2CA connection factories:

- One is local and directly accesses IMS Connect using MVS™ cross-memory.
- The other is remote and accesses IMS Connect using TCP/IP.

The IMS Resource Adapter is the J2CA implementation of the connector to access IMS. J2CA has standardized the Java classes needed by an application to access an Enterprise Information System (EIS), such as IMS. J2CA defines the contracts between the application, the connector, and the application server where the application will be deployed.

Note: The IMS Resource Adapter is included in WebSphere Studio Application Developer Integration Edition for development. The IMS Resource Adapter run time is provided separately for deployment to WebSphere Application Server. The IMS Resource Adapter run time is available for download from the IMS Web site. If an update is necessary for the IMS Resource Adapter, it is made available as an IFix to WebSphere Studio Application Developer Integration Edition. The corresponding updated run time is available for download from the IMS Web site.

You should ensure that both the development and run times of the IMS resource adapter are coordinated by applying the IFix to WebSphere Studio Application Developer Integration Edition and redeploying the updated run time to WebSphere Application Server.

Chapter 4. IMS connectivity options   **99**

4.2 Interface components: IMS Connect

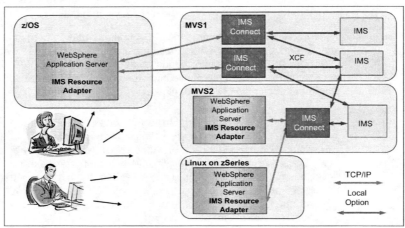

Figure 4-2   IMS Connect

IMS Connect in Figure 4-2 provides e-business access to new and existing IMS applications as well as operations. It supports communications between one or more TCP/IP or local z/OS clients and one or more IMS systems.

IMS Connect architecture is designed to support any clients communicating with socket calls. One of the clients of IMS Connect is IMS Connector for Java, which is a collection of Java classes that enable a Java application to communicate data requests to IMS Connect.

IMS Connect also supports the Local Option connection which is a non-TCP/IP connection between IMS Connect and the IMS Resource Adapter (IMS Connector for Java) deployed in WebSphere Application Server for z/OS.

IMS Connect executes on an OS/390 or z/OS environment and allows TCP/IP clients or local z/OS clients to send messages to IMS. IMS Connect uses the IMS Open Transaction Manager Access (OTMA) interface and the MVS Cross Coupling Facility (XCF) to communicate with IMS. Table 4-1 on page 101 shows the functional differences between a local and remote connections.

Table 4-1   Function list comparison for IMS Connect in local and remote modes.

Function	TCP/IP	Local
two-phase commit	XA	RRS
executionTimeout	Yes	No
SSL	Yes	N/A
Commit Mode 1	Yes	Yes
Commit Mode 0 on shareable	Yes	No CM0 not supported with Local Option
Commit Mode 0 on dedicated	Yes	No. CM0 not supported with Local Option
Connection Retry	Yes	No, N/A
SEND_ONLY	Yes	No
socketTimeout	Yes	No, N/A

4.3 Local IMS connection

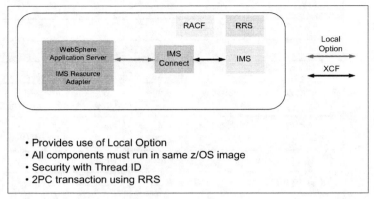

Figure 4-3   Local connection

IMS Connect provides for a Local Option support, as in Figure 4-3. Local Option support is a means of communicating from WebSphere for z/OS to IMS Connect through the Resource Adapter.

Local Option provides non-socket, an Multiple Virtual Storage (MVS) program call, access to IMS transactions and data from the Application Server when Websphere, IMS Connector for Java, and IMS Connect are all running in the *same* MVS image.

The Local Option also supports two-phase commit using RRS.

If Websphere Application Server and IMS Connect are on the same z/OS image, you can use either the Local Option or TCP/IP.

4.3.1 Local IMS connection: Attributes

Performance
- Best option for performance
- Uses a Program Call protocol
- RRS performs better in local environment

Availability
- No failover provided
- Consider ARM to decrease outage time

Security
- RACF is used for this configuration
- Thread Identity available for local resources via Websphere

Transactionality
- RRS compliant for 2PC
- Uses WebSphere global transaction support
- Conversational and non-conversational supported

Scalability
- No automatic growth

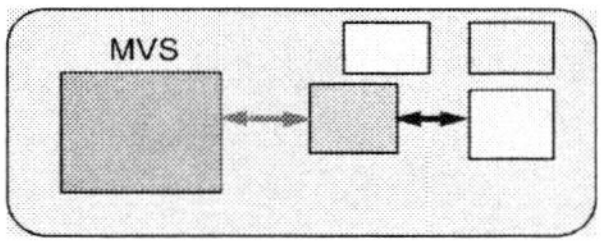

Figure 4-4   Local connection attributes

Performance

Use the Local Option for highest throughput and performance. It uses a non-network communication method to access IMS. This provides a tight integration between the application server and the IMS subsystem because there is no networking involved. See Figure 4-4.

When you execute a global transaction with Local Option, WebSphere, IMS Connector for Java, IMS Connect and RRS must all reside in the same z/OS image. In this case, the WebSphere Application Server for z/OS Transaction Manager exploits RRS to coordinate the transaction, rather than using the XA protocol with TCP/IP. RRS should provide a performance benefit over TCP/IP using the XA protocol.

Availability

Although local connections to IMS subsystems provide better performance, there are other considerations. When accessing an EIS subsystem locally, there is no fail-over. You are not managing the workload for this connection. As a result, if the local subsystem goes down, your connection is not going to be routed to another system in the sysplex.

If you need workload balancing between Websphere Application Server and EIS subsystems, you should consider using a remote connection through one of the various mechanisms described later.

The status of the IMS database is sent to IMS Connect from OTMA through XCF. If the data store goes down, IMS Connect is notified and automatically reconnects to the data store when it is restarted. You do not need to manually reconnect to the data store.

This option has the least availability since each point of interaction can be subject to failure. You can automate monitors to ensure each server component is executing as expected.

The Automatic Restart Manager (ARM) can be considered to decrease the outage time in a production IMS.

Security

The IMS Resource Adapter passes the security information, user ID and optional group name, that it receives from WebSphere to IMS Connect in an OTMA message. WebSphere Application Server works this way using the Local Option with container-managed sign-on:

► IMS Connect does not call SAF because authentication takes place when the application server generated the UTOKEN, an encapsulated version of the security information of an authenticated user. If IMS Connect is configured to use RACF, it will authenticate every request unless the exits are used to enable Trusted Client support.

► WebSphere can be configured to implement the Thread Identity relating to the execution thread of the Servant region to authenticate a user. The Application Server creates and passes the UTOKEN to the IMS resource adapter, which forwards the token to IMS Connect for sign-on to the IMS.

The thread identity function is only available in those configurations where J2CA connectors (or JDBC providers) access local z/OS resources through callable (not TCP/IP) interfaces. IMS provides thread identity support only if the target IMS is configured on the same system as the z/OS Websphere Application Server and is accessed via a Local connection.

If <res-auth>Container/res-auth> is specified in the deployment descriptor, container-managed EIS sign-on is used. Your application does not have to programmatically provide security information. It is provided by the application server.

Note: If you provide an authentication alias, it will be used by default.

Transactional capabilities

Websphere Application Server uses RRS with an extension incorporating the J2EE Connector Architecture (J2CA) resource adapter specification, supporting transaction processing.

The local configuration is the only configuration in which IMS Connector for Java runs as an RRS-transactional connector.

To use transaction support with IMS Connector for Java, use either the JTA transaction interface, or set an appropriate transaction attribute in the deployment descriptor (for example, TX_REQUIRED) in your application. You can have conversational and non-conversational transaction capability.

The resource adapter, when running global transactions with the Local Option, does not use the X/Open (XA) protocol.

If there is an error during processing, both IMS and WebSphere Application Server for z/OS rely on the underlying RRS subsystem to handle all rollback. In the case of inflight transactions, RRS notifies all participants that a rollback is required and normal rollback processing occurs.

Scalability

Although it is not shown, you can have more than one IMS Connect within an LPAR for connector scalability. However, a single IMS Connect can handle a high transaction volume, therefore multiple instances of IMS Connect are not usually required for scalability.

4.4 Local IMS connection in the same sysplex

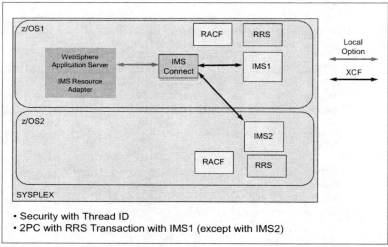

Figure 4-5   Local connection same sysplex

In Figure 4-5 we have a similar architecture as in Figure 4-4 on page 103, except for the introduction of a remote IMS (z/OS2) within the same sysplex.

A single IMS Connect can support one or multiple IMS systems. Multiple IMS Connects can be used to access one IMS system. An IMS Connect system can reside on the same LPAR image as its target IMS, or can cross a system boundary, assuming that the environment is sysplex-enabled.

IMS Connect uses XCF to talk to the local IMS1 and uses XCF and the Coupling Facility to talk to the remote IMS2. The client in both cases is WebSphere Application Server.

This configuration can implement message queue sharing. This support allows multiple IMS subsystems to share the same IMS full-function message queues and the same Fast Path Expedited Message Handler (EMH) queues. Sharing of the same message queue between multiple IMS subsystems provides fuller exploitation of the power of the Parallel Sysplex, providing workload balancing and increased availability.

4.4.1 Local IMS connection in same sysplex: Attributes

Performance
- Single IMS Connect supports a very high transaction rate
- Cost in using shared data queues

Availability
- Shared message queues for IMS and multiple IMS Connect address spaces
- IMS Connect is a single point of failure

Security
- Thread Identity (RunAs) Identity for local connection
- RACF setting in IMS Connect used to set authorization.
- User Message Exit can be implemented for security authentication

Transactionality
- RRS Compliant for 2PC in local LPAR
- XA Compliant for 2PC in remote LPAR
- Uses WebSphere global transaction support

Scalability
- Shared queues can be used with multiple IMS LPARs

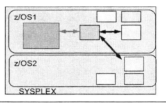

Figure 4-6   Local connection in same sysplex: Attributes

Performance

A single IMS Connect, as in Figure 4-6, can be configured to support a very high transaction rate. In this scenario there are two separate IMS systems residing in different LPARs within the same Sysplex, a combination of local and remote processing. The local service time will have better response than the remote because inter-LPAR communication is not involved.

There is a cost to data-sharing with shared message queues. The performance costs that arise from exercising the Parallel Sysplex functions are variable. Hardware configurations and workload characteristics, such as the amount of sharing required by applications, are all factors in the evaluation of the performance of customer environments.

> **Tip:** A best practice for configuring IMS Connect for multiple IMS instances for performance is to segregate the ports for each IMS. Do not send the request for different IMS systems along the same port.

Availability

This scenario contains a number of single points of failure. If LPAR1, the Websphere Application Server in it, or IMS Connect fails, then both IMS systems are affected.

For availability, several IMS Connects can be configured to communicate with multiple IMS systems within a sysplex.

Use shared message queues by using the Coupling Facility list structures. If one IMS subsystem fails, the rest of the IMS subsystems sharing the message queues can continue to process work, including any message placed on the shared queues by the failed IMS subsystem. IMS Connect and the IMS datastore must be in the same XCF Group in order to communicate.

> **Note:** The IMS Connect User Message Exits provide an interface that allows you an opportunity to customize a solution for fail-over and load balancing.
>
> Refer to the *IMS Connect Guide and Reference Version 2 Release 2,* SC18-7260 for more information on the message exits.

Security

Websphere Application Server for z/OS allows you to assign a thread identifier as an owner of a Local connection (IMS1), when you first obtain the connection. In terms of thread identity we refer to the J2EE Identity, the *RunAs* Identity, for example.

When you use the Local Option and IMS Connect is configured to use RACF, it will authenticate every request unless the exits are used to enable trusted user support.

Another means of security verification, other than using RACF password, is using a PassTicket. You use a PassTicket to authenticate user IDs and log on to application systems that communicate with RACF. You can select PassTicket support through an IMS Connect client and send a PassTicket in the IRM in place of a RACF password.

See 4.8, "IMS security flow: Container-managed" on page 120 for more information

Transactional capabilities

Websphere Application Server supports the coordination of resource managers through their RRS and XA Resource interface and participates in distributed global transactions with other Object Transaction Service (OTS) 1.2-compliant transaction managers.

Websphere uses signals from RRS to drive subordinate OTS nodes during a distributed transaction. Websphere applications can be configured to interact with databases through their local transaction support when distributed transaction coordination is not required.

Websphere Application Server for z/OS is capable of coordinating a mix of RRS transactional resource managers and XA-capable resource managers under the same global transaction.

IMS Connect is a multiple role player in two-phase commit processing. IMS Connect acts as an extension to RRS and is considered the extended distributed syncpoint manager. Therefore, if you use global transaction support and IMS as well as Websphere server reside on different MVS images, you must use TCP/IP protocol, although RRS and IMS Connect must be located in same LPAR.

If you want to use global transaction support and your IMS and Websphere Application Server are on different MVS images, you *must* use TCP/IP as your communication protocol.

RRS support is only applicable in a local environment where the back-end IMS Connect resides on the same system, therefore the XA protocol is not used by IMS Connector for Java when running a global transaction with Local Option.

Scalability

As mentioned earlier, a single IMS Connect can sustain a high transaction rate and therefore scalability may not be required. Implementing shared message queuing, a message placed on the shared queue can be processed by any IMS in the Sysplex, thus increasing capacity.

4.5 Local IMS connection: High availability

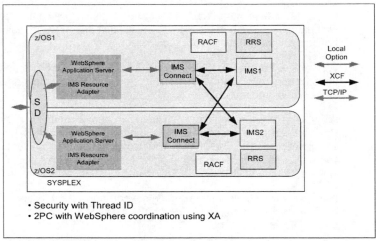

Figure 4-7   Local connection with high availability

This scenario in Figure 4-7 shows a high availability WebSphere cluster with local connections to IMS Connect. Each WebSphere cluster member can talk to a single IMS Connect. This can cause availability problems, in fact the storm drain can happen if IMS Connect goes down. The IMS Connect can talk to a shared queue to get to multiple IMS servers.

Local connection means that all local security benefits like thread indentity apply. On the other hand the local IMS connection has less features than the remote TCP/IP.

4.5.1 Local IMS connection with availability: Attributes

Performance
- Single IMS Connect supports a very high transaction rate
- Cost in using shared data queues

Availability
- Shared message queues for IMS and multiple IMS Connect address spaces
- IMS Connect is a single point of failure

Security
- Thread Identity (RunAs) Identity for local connection
- RACF setting in IMS Connect used to set authorization.
- User Message Exit can be implemented for security authentication

Transactional capabilities
- RRS Compliant for 2PC in local LPAR
- XA Compliant for 2PC in remote LPAR
- Uses WebSphere global transaction support

Scalability
- Increasing the number of WebSphere cluster members and IMS Connects

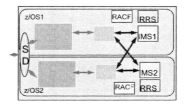

Figure 4-8   Local connection with availability: Attributes

Performance

A single IMS Connect can be configured to support a very high transaction rate. In this scenario we have two separate IMS systems residing in different LPARs within the same Sysplex, a combination of local and remote processing. The local service time will have better response than the remote since inter-LPAR communication is not involved. See Figure 4-6.

There is a cost to data sharing with shared message queues. The performance costs that arise from exercising the Parallel Sysplex functions are variable. Hardware configurations and workload characteristics, such as the amount of sharing required by applications, are all factors in the evaluation of the performance of customer environments.

> **Tip:** A best practice for performance is configuring IMS Connect for multiple IMS instances is to segregate the ports for each IMS. Do not send the request for different IMS systems through the same port.

Availability

To increase availability, several IMS Connects can be configured to communicate with multiple IMS systems within a sysplex.

This scenario contains a single point of failure. If in LPAR1 or 2 IMS Connect fails, WebSphere does not detect and it does not report very fast response times to WLM. This tells the sysplex distributor to send more work to WebSphere, which results in the storm drain effect. But the probability of IMS Connect failing in the LPAR is very small, making this clustered solution considered to be highly available.

Use shared message queues by using the Coupling Facility list structures. If one IMS subsystem fails, the rest of the IMS subsystems sharing the message queues can continue to process work, including any message placed on the shared queues by the failed IMS subsystem. IMS Connect and the IMS datastore must be in the same XCF Group in order to communicate.

Security

As WebSphere and IMS Connect have local connection, they can benefit from the thread identity support. Thread Identity support is used to flow the current thread identity to the back-end IMS Connect and IMS. Most z/OS customers will want to use this feature because it enables WebSphere for z/OS to behave in a way that traditional z/OS address spaces behave, that is, once you have authenticated, your user ID flows with any work you do within the z/OS system.

Thread Identity in WebSphere for z/OS applies only to container-managed connections. It allows the container to pass the security identity of the current Java thread to the J2CA connector and then to IMS.

Transactional capabilities

The transactional attributes of this scenario are the same as Section 4.4.1, "Local IMS connection in same sysplex: Attributes" on page 107.

Scalability

This architecture uses WebSphere clusters, multiple IMS Connects and multiple IMS servers to enhance scalability. Implementing shared message queuing, a message placed on the shared queue can be processed by any IMS in the Sysplex, increasing capacity.

112   WebSphere for z/OS Connectivity Architectural Choices

4.6 Remote IMS in same sysplex: Availability

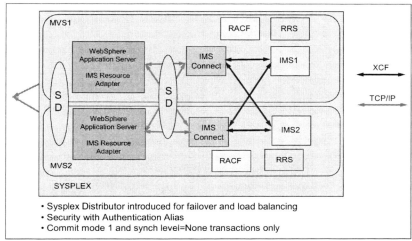

Figure 4-9   Remote connection with availability

In Figure 4-9, we placed the Sysplex Distributor as the means for spreading the WebSphere cluster workload over two LPARs ,targeting multiple back-end IMS systems.

This provides redundancy to carry on processing the workload if one node, LPAR, fails. Furthermore, you can recycle a server clone after configuration changes without taking the whole cluster down.

A fully redundant architecture in each LPAR supports most failover conditions. This architecture is commonly seen on the z/OS platform. The application server tier resides on two nodes spread over two different LPARs in a Sysplex.

A failure of one node leaves the servers on the other nodes able to continue processing the workload and provide a system from which to restart the failing application server, if required.

The transactional capabilities of this solution are very limited, because sysplex distributor does not necessarily routes the recovery request to the same IMS Connect as the original transaction.

4.6.1 Remote connection with availability: Attributes

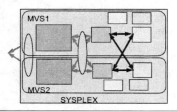

Performance
- Not as good as local
- Use shared message queues for performance

Availability
- This is a common topology for z/OS
- SD integrates availability management
- Use of shared message queues for availability
- Apps must use sharable persistent sockets
- Only synchronous output can be retrieved

Security
- Since alternate paths can take place, the User Message Exit for IMS Connect and shared RACF can simplify security
- Thread ID cannot be used
- Use JAAS authentication

Transactionality
- Commit mode 1 only (Send-then-commit) – IMS sends the reply and then commits the transaction
- Synch level = none only – No acknowledgement

Scalability
- Multiple SDs provided growth horizontally between LPARs for IMS transactions

Figure 4-10   Availability configuration: Attributes

Performance
We recommend that if you are using a sysplex, set up your TCP/IP network with Sysplex Distributor, as in Figure 4-6. This makes use of dynamic virtual IP addresses (DVIPAs) and allows workload balancing, which can help with overall performance.

The IMS Multi System Coupling (MSC) facility provides reliable, high bandwidth host-to-host communication support between IMS Systems. It provides FICON® Channel-To-Channel (CTC) support enabling higher throughput between processors. IMS MSC FICON CTC support increases the volume of IMS messages that can go between IMS Systems.

The IMS Write Ahead Data Set (WADS) feature using FICON can perform channel command prefetching to increase execution speed for the channels.

Availability
The objective of this configuration is high availability, eliminating single points of failure. Each of the data store access paths has redundancy to support any failure. This architecture is commonly seen on z/OS platforms.

The Application Server resides on two separate nodes spread over two different LPARs in the parallel sysplex. Even with an outage of an LPAR, Websphere Server, IMS Connect or IMS Database, servers on the alternate LPAR can continue processing the workload.

The Sysplex Distributor is positioned in two strategic locations to ensure optimal resource availability. Prior to Websphere, it selects the most appropriate Application Server instance to route the client request for web processing, then the Sysplex Distributor is invoked a second time to ensure availability of the database instance to forward on the transaction.

When provided with access to multiple IMS systems, code can be added to the IMS Connect user message exits to perform further load balancing and failover if redundant IMS Connects are implemented within an LPAR. IMS Connect provides a datastore table that keeps track of the status, active or inactive, of all the IMS systems that are defined in a configuration file. The table is updated as events occur. When a message reaches IMS Connect, an appropriate user message exit is invoked. All user message exits have access to the datastore table, and can take action based upon the information.

The IMS Connect user message exit is enhanced to verify that the IMS system, as defined by the datastore ID, is available. If the target IMS is available, then the exit makes no changes to the destination. If it is not available, then the exit can implement a failover solution by routing the message to another, active IMS system.

The IMS Connect user message exits provide an interface that allows a creative programmer the opportunity to code a solution that answers both a failover and a load balancing need.

> **Note:** There can be multiple IMS Connects in a sysplex within multiple IMS images using a shared queue for availability, assuming all IMS images can handle any relevant request.

Security

For multiple LPAR connectivity using TCP/IP, either a component-managed or container-managed alias is determined by the Res-Auth setting in the deployment descriptor and not the RACF setting in the IMS Connect configuration.

Remote Identity support should be implemented since transaction paths can vary, depending resource availability.

For a remote IMS using TCP/IP, the application server passes the security information in the JAAS alias to the resource adapter. It then passes the security

Chapter 4. IMS connectivity options   **115**

information to IMS Connect for authentication and finally passes it to IMS for sign-on. If IMS Connect cannot authenticate the user, a security failure is returned to the IMS resource adapter, passing an exception to the application.

Also for the remote connection, TCP/IP sockets, running in a Websphere environment, SSL (Java Secure Socket Extension) communication can be implemented between the IMS Connector for Java, the resource adapter, and IMS Connect using a combination of public and private keys with symmetric key encryption schemes. If you use SSL, consider a tool for key management so that you can add or delete certificates. The adapter does not require a specific key management tool for SSL support.

See 4.8, "IMS security flow: Container-managed" on page 120 for more information.

Transactional capabilities

This scenario limits transactional capabilities. While on the front, the HTTP server plug-in (not shown on Figure 4-9 on page 113) does affinity processing and the sysplex distributor is not involved when affinity is established, the second sysplex distributor is always involved. This means that sysplex distributor can route anywhere between the two IMS Connects and the two IMS Connects each do not know the state of the other.

This limits this solution to applications using Commit Mode 1, send-then-commit, and Sync Level=None. The request is sent to IMS. It sends back the reply, commits the transaction and, not checking whether the reply arrived or not, commits.

Scalability

This configuration provides for the ultimate in horizontal scalability using a combination of WebSphere front and back door Sysplex Distributors for availability and load-balancing between the isolated IMS resource managers.

4.7 Remote IMS in different sysplexes

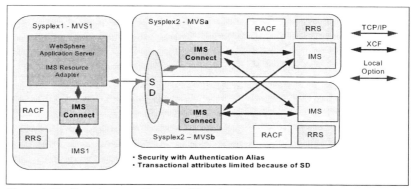

Figure 4-11   Remote connection with different sysplexes

In Figure 4-11 we show a Multi-Sysplex IMS configuration. A single Websphere Application Server instance, Sysplex1, is the hub communicating to multiple IMS systems in both local and remote images, Sysplex1 and Sysplex2. Each LPAR contains an IMS Connect interfacing with their respective IMS data stores. The IMS Connects can talk to both IMSs through XCF.

In this configuration, the Websphere Application Server can become the bottleneck for throughput while servicing multiple IMS systems and the single point of failure for the topology.

Since a single IMS Connect can manage a very high transaction rate. The configuration within Sysplex2 provides redundant components, allowing load-balancing and failover.

Although sysplex distributor solves the failover and workload balancing, it causes problems with the transaction management because it can spray requests to any IMS Connect.

4.7.1 Remote IMS in different sysplexes: Attributes

Performance
- Performance better for local IMS
- Use of shared message queues for performance

Availability
- WebSphere is a single point of failure
- Sysplex2 provides availability management

Security
- Can use thread identity for local IMS
- Use JAAS authentication for remote

Transactional capabilities
- Two phase commit is available for local IMS
- Commit mode 1 and syncpoint=none for remote IMS

Scalability
- SD in Sysplex2 provided growth horizontally between LPARs for IMS transactions
- Sysplex1 has no automatic growth capability

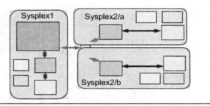

Figure 4-12 Remote connection different sysplexes: Attributes

Performance

Overall performance management is more challenging since there are two Sysplexes and three LPARs. See Figure 4-12. Each Sysplex has a separate Workload Management Policy, other mixed workloads are among the IMS systems executing on the images.

For Sysplex2, the Sysplex Distributor has the ability to specify certain policies within the Policy Agent enforcing Quality of Service (QoS) to the target stack and WLM server load, ensuring these policies specify which target stacks are candidates in a particular sub-network. In this case, a network interface between the two Sysplexes will be negotiated and monitored to ensure Service Level Objectives (SLO) are attained.

Availability

Because Websphere Application Server for z/OS is a single point of control for database application connectivity, WebSphere is the critical component in this scenario. If WebSphere Application Server fails, so does the connectivity to all IMS systems that are participating in this architecture.

In Sysplex1, if either IMS Connect or IMS fails, the run time for these applications also fails. There is no failover for this environment. This configuration takes on all attributes of the Local Option discussed earlier.

In Sysplex2, the Sysplex Distributor is implemented, therefore have the ability to provide for redundant components to ensure failover capability. It also offers load-distribution, combining routing technology used for the distribution of incoming connections to ensure high availability for service within the sysplex. The Sysplex Distributor works with Domain Name Services and WLM to determine server load. It informs the communication stack of resource availability so that the stack may make the optimal intelligent decision of where to send the incoming request.

Security

If there is a shared RACF between the LPARs in Sysplex2, ThreadID (UToken) should work correctly. Container Managed sign-on can be used between Sysplexes. It passes the password credential containing the security information from the authenticated alias in the Connection Factory.

See 4.8, "IMS security flow: Container-managed" on page 120 for more information.

Transactional capabilities

A combination of one- and two-phase commit can be implemented, although distributed two-phase commit should be used with high caution.

Scalability

The scaling within Sysplex1 is limited to the number of servant address spaces inside Websphere Application Server that are capable of spawning. Within the Administrative Console for Websphere, along with WLM, there is a panel that governs the number of servants that can be created. Consider a high-water mark for creating servants. This protects capacity planning.

In Sysplex2, the scaling of workload is enhanced as a function of the Sysplex Distributor to determine which IMS within that Sysplex has resources to met the workload goal. This is not necessarily a true form of scaling, but is mentioned here because resource management for each LPAR in Sysplex2 can vary, depending on concurrent workload of the competing transaction mix.

Chapter 4. IMS connectivity options   **119**

4.8 IMS security flow: Container-managed

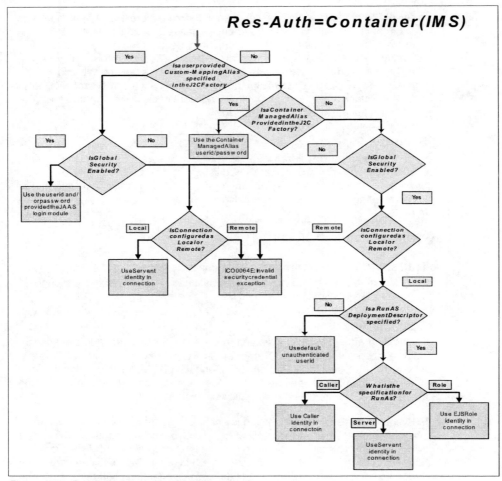

Figure 4-13   Detailed container managed security flow

Figure 4-13 shows the detailed security options available when the container is managing the connection and security. The used identity is dependent on a number of items, such as:

- Custom Login module used
- Global security is enabled
- JAAS entry created
- Remote or Local connection
- RunAs deployment option specified

The above security flow is provided here for reference. For more details see *WebSphere for z/OS Connectivity Handbook*, SG24-7064.

4.9 IMS security flow: Component-managed

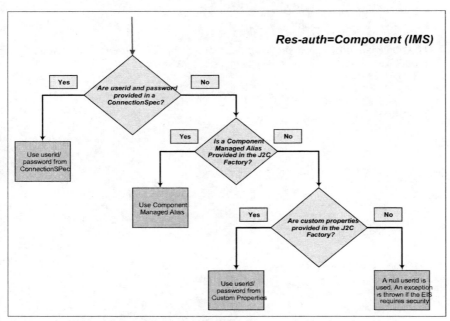

Figure 4-14   Component-managed security flow

Figure 4-14 shows the detailed security options available when the application or component is managing the connection and security. The used identity is, as in the Component-managed case, dependent on a number of items.

The above security flow is provided here for reference, for more details see *WebSphere for z/OS Connectivity Handbook,* SG24-7064.

4.10 JDBC for IMS

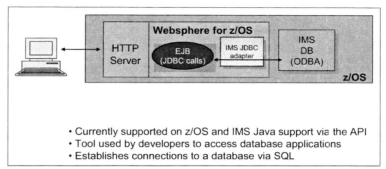

Figure 4-15   JDBC access to IMS DB data

In Figure 4-15, JDBC access to IMS DB or IMS DB/TM for Websphere EJB applications use the ODBA interface. You can write WebSphere EJBs to access IMS databases through the JDBC API. The IMS Java classes use the ODBA interface to IMS.

The JDBC interface provides a known way of doing business for the database developer and the possibility of composing database applications using a pure Java API. JDBC enables the writing of a single program using the JDBC API. The program is able to send SQL statements to the appropriate database. JDBC allows an application to establish a connection with a database, send SQL statements and process the result set.

IMS V7 first provided JDBC access to IMS DB. For IMS V8 the IMS Java Classes are updated to support some of the Optional APIs and JDBC 2.0 Core classes.

Normally, database programming design allows for two styles. The first style utilizes JDBC and provides higher-level access designed for Java programmers who might not be familiar with IMS. The second style is more closely associated with current IMS application programming and provides lower-level access to most IMS functions. Both of these mechanisms are built upon classes that the code developer provides for defining the segments and segment hierarchies available to the application. We recommend that you use the higher-level style.

IMS does not support the local, connection-based commit scope defined in the JDBC model. Therefore, the DL/I implementation of Connection.commit, Connection.rollback and Connection.setAutoCommit result in an SQLException when called from a client program.

SQL does not provide the ability to insert multiple rows, segment occurrences, and multiple tables, segment types, on one insert call. This means the IMS Java Classes cannot provide a path insert DL/I call when using JDBC SQL interface.

> **Note:** IMS uses Segment Search Arguments (SSA), not SQL. IMS uses an internal SQL-to-SSA parser.

The IMS JDBC connection factories support the assignment of the identity associated with the current thread as the owner of a connection for authentication purposes when global security is enabled. The assignment is performed when the following conditions are met:

- ► Container-managed resource authority (res-auth=Container) is specified in the application deployment descriptors.
- ► Connection Manager RunAs Identity is enabled.

WebSphere Application Server for z/OS allows JDBC providers to define the level of thread identity support for defined data sources and connection factories. JDBC providers only make this available for local z/OS resources through a callable interface. There is no TCP/IP solution for IMS JDBC.

Caching of connection handles across servlet methods is limited to JDBC. Other non-relational resources, such as IMS, currently cannot have their connection handles cached in a servlet. You need to get, use, and close the connection handle within each method invocation. This limitation only applies to single-threaded servlets because multi-threaded servlets do not allow caching of connection handles.

124 WebSphere for z/OS Connectivity Architectural Choices

5

WebSphere MQ connectivity options

This chapter provides topology options for connecting WebSphere Application Server for z/OS to WebSphere MQ. This chapter describes basic scenarios:

- ► Connecting to a local WebSphere MQ (Binding mode)
- ► Connecting to a remote WebSphere MQ (Client mode)
- ► Using WebSphere MQ cluster, queue sharing, and bridge functions

5.1 Local MQ connectivity: Bindings mode

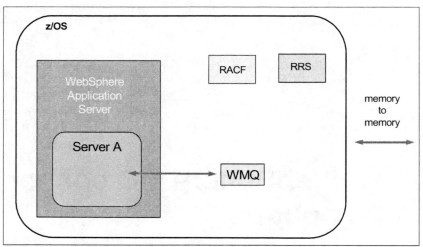

Figure 5-1   Local connectivity to WebSphere MQ

in Figure 5-1, WebSphere MQ provides native code which allows cross-memory communication to WebSphere Application Server. This transport type for Java Message Service (JMS) is called *binding mode,* or local connection.

The Queue Manager (WebSphere MQ) and WebSphere Application Server must both exist on the same z/OS image.

Binding mode supports transactional applications by using a WebSphere Application Server stub, CSQBWSTB, which uses RRS services.

For more information see the WebSphere MQ library, most notably *MQSeries Using Java,*SC34-5456.

5.1.1 Binding mode: Attributes

```
* Performance
    ▸ Best option for performance
    ▸ Uses a Program Call protocol
    ▸ RRS performs better in local environment
* Availability
    ▸ No failover provided
    ▸ Consider ARM to decrease outage time
* Scalability
    ▸ by adding additional servers (using WLM)
    ▸ provided by zSeries architecture - scales vertically
* Security
    ▸ RACF can be used for this configuration
    ▸ Thread Identity available for local resources via Websphere
* Transactional capabilites
    ▸ RRS compliant for 2PC
    ▸ Uses WebSphere global transaction support
* Considerations
    ▸ All components must reside in same z/OS image
```

Figure 5-2   Binding mode attributes for WebSphere MQ

Performance

Use the Binding mode for highest throughput and performance. See Figure 5-2. There are no delays due to network connections, because communication is performed on the memory level by native code between the application server and WebSphere MQ residing on the same z/OS image.

Availability

Failover options are limited with this configuration. There is no failover between an individual WebSphere servant region and a WebSphere MQ server if either fails. The only possibilities you have to increase availability are the use of multiple servants, running the same application or cluster, and the use of several queue managers. If there is a failure of the WebSphere MQ server this scenario is prone to the storm drain. To avoid this, use system automation tools like Netview.

In this configuration, availability is provided mainly by the traditional zSeries hardware and z/OS reliability. For fast recovery use ARM.

Chapter 5. WebSphere MQ connectivity options   **127**

Scalability

The local configuration lacks in horizontal scalability because it is designed to satisfy the requirements of a single installation.

To scale the solution, additional WebSphere server regions should be used. Manage them with WLM for optimal resource allocation.

The system can be vertically scaled by increasing CPU capacity (number, speed), memory, channels and other zSeries resources.

Security

The level of security in this configuration is good.

Normally, when a user attempts to access a WebSphere MQ resource, RACF checks the relevant user ID or IDs to see if access is allowed to that resource.

When using a binding mode connection, you do not need to be concerned about establishing trust of requests from WebSphere for z/OS, but you might still require authorization control for WebSphere MQ resources.

WebSphere Application Server linked to WebSphere MQ provides the thread identity function, meaning the WebSphere application server passes a User ID to WebSphere MQ with each connection request.

The thread identity function is only available in those server configurations where local z/OS resources are accessed through callable (not TCP/IP) interfaces.

Specific security options include the use of container and component-managed authentication aliases, server region identity, get connection (Universal Identifiyer (UID) and PW) support, and SAF profiles to control access to WebSphere MQ resources.

Transactional capabilities

The binding configuration scenario allows the realization of 2PC processing, using a WebSphere Application Server stub, CSQBWSTB, which uses the RRS facility.

This and the use of WebSphere Application Server global transaction support guarantee a high level of transaction management.

5.2 Remote MQ connectivity: Client mode

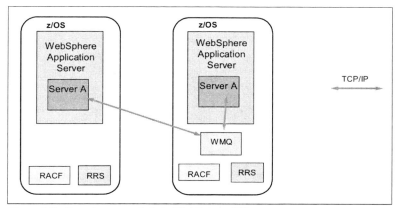

Figure 5-3   Remote connectivity to WebSphere MQ

If you prefer to separate WebSphere Application Server and WebSphere MQ, as in Figure 5-3, and have them on separate LPARs for software cost or isolation reasons, binding mode (cross-memory communication) is not available.

WebSphere MQ provides remote connection support through TCP/IP. This transport type for JMS is called *client* mode. It supports transactional applications by using XA protocols.

If WebSphere MQ and WebSphere Application Server exist on the same z/OS image, you could use client mode as well. Binding mode is recommended for performance and security reasons.

5.2.1 Client mode: Attributes

- Performance
  - communication via TCP/IP across LPARs means network traffic which reduces performance
- Availability
  - Is worse than a single LPAR, by having two single point of failures
  - Consider ARM to decrease outage time
- Scalability
  - Is the same as Binding mode. You can add CPs to the LPARs. Having 2 LPARs means independent scalability on the 2 LPARs
- Security
  - No Thread Security for accessing WMQ, but can use Container or Component managed JAAS alias and RACF profiles
- Transactionality
  - XA support for global transactions provided by WebSphere/JMS

Figure 5-4   Client mode attributes for WebSphere MQ

Performance

Using the client mode decreases performance in comparison to binding mode as an additional layer, the network, is involved in communication. See Figure 5-4. Requests from WebSphere Application Server have to pass through two TCP/IP stacks and a network to reach WebSphere MQ resources. Even if the remote connection can be improved by the use of zSeries facilities to reduce TCP/IP delays, the local connection will always perform better.

Availability

Failover options are limited with this configuration. There is no failover between an individual WebSphere servant region and a WebSphere MQ server if either fails. The possibilities you have are:

- Running the application in a WebSphere cluster
- Running multiple queue managers

To reduce the risk of storm drain, use system automation tools like Netview.In a parallel sysplex, you can use queue sharing for WebSphere MQ. From a total system point of view, there are more points of possible failure: WebSphere, the network, and two z/OS images.

In this configuration, availability is provided mainly by the traditional zSeries hardware and z/OS reliability. For fast recovery, use ARM.

130   WebSphere for z/OS Connectivity Architectural Choices

Scalability

The scalability for remote configuration is limited by a finite number of additional WebSphere servants. WebSphere MQ can be scaled by adding more queue managers (defining the MQ resources) on either LPAR. Use WLM for better resource allocation and Sysplex Distributor for load-balancing.

The system can be vertically scaled by increasing CPU capacity (number, speed), memory, channels and other zSeries resources. Overall scalability is similar to the binding mode connectivity.

Security

What differentiates this configuration from the binding mode is the connection of the JMS client in WebSphere Application Server to the Queue Manager being established through the Channel Initiator address space using a special channel, SERVCON. There is also a fundamental change with the binding mode in that the user ID provided by the application with the getConnection() function is now honored.

Therefore you have to protect three layers in addition to the WebSphere Application Server: the WebSphere MQ resources themselves, the transport layer and the applications accessed by WebSphere MQ.

The protection of the WebSphere MQ resources is addressed by WebSphere MQ itself, which implements internally the proper calls to an external security manager, through the SAF interface (RACF).

The transport level security has to be set up in the transport mechanism itself, for the purpose of authentication at the end points, and the integrity and privacy of exchanged data, if required. This is typically covered by using secure protocols such as SSL or IPSec to protect the flow of data.

WebSphere Application Server provides the component or container-managed Authentication Aliases. These user ID and password pairs can be used to provide authentication data to WebSphere MQ.

Transactional capabilities

The remote configuration scenario allows the realization of two-phase commit processing, using XA protocols with the RRS facility.

In a WebSphere Application Server environment, the semantics of the JMS session object determine whether single-phase or two-phase commit coordination is used. WebSphere MQ can either be the participant or the coordinator in the transaction.

Chapter 5. WebSphere MQ connectivity options   **131**

5.3 WebSphere MQ connectivity with availability

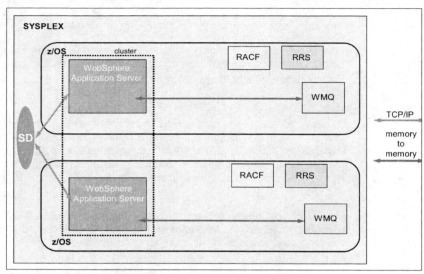

Figure 5-5   Addressing WebSphere scalability and availability

The configuration in Figure 5-5 combines the performance advantages of the local connection between WebSphere Application Server and WebSphere MQ and the availability and scalability advantages provided by the Sysplex environment and the Sysplex Distributor.

There are no delays due to network connections, because communication is done on the memory level by native code between WebSphere Application Server and WebSphere MQ residing on the same z/OS image.

A little extra network traffic might arise due to the additional component, the Sysplex Distributor, which allows DVIPA and routes the client requests to the appropriate WebSphere Application Server in the Sysplex, providing load balancing and checking on availability as well.

Sysplex Distributor uses WLM performance data and its own algorithms to select which application server in the sysplex is best suited to service a request. This is only for non-affinity cases, session affinity is not handled by sysplex distributor. Refer to *Enabling High Availability e-Business on IBM eServer zSeries*, SG24-6850-01.

There is no failover between an individual WebSphere servant region and a WebSphere MQ server if either fails. You can increase availability through the use of multiple Servants, running the same application (cluster), and the use of several queue managers.

If there is a failure of the WebSphere MQ queue manager a storm drain is possible. To avoid this, use system automation tools such as Netview, which can automatically stop the application server if the queue manager fails. For fast, recovery use z/OS facilities like ARM.

This scenario provides additional backup because of the Sysplex environment. If WebSphere Application Server or WebSphere MQ fail on one system, the second system still provides the functionary as all requests are routed to it by the Sysplex Distributor.

5.4 Increasing availability with shared queues

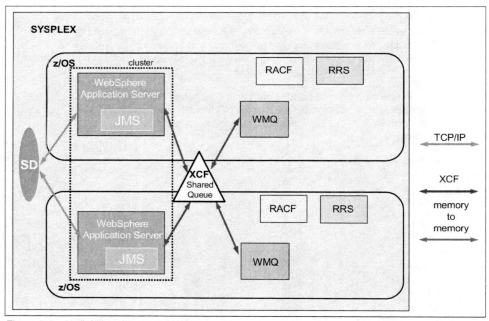

Figure 5-6   Availability with shared queues

WebSphere MQ availability can be addressed by using shared queues. The loss of a single WebSphere MQ server does not mean the loss of all messages for a particular WebSphere server. The messages are written to a shared queue as in Figure 5-6. The remaining WebSphere MQ server can still process them.

Use this configuration if availability is of highest importance to you and you can live with slightly decreased performance in comparison to the configuration shown in Figure 5-5 on page 132.

Additional availability is gained here due to the use of shared queues. An application in WebSphere Application Server can connect to any of the queue managers within the queue-sharing group. Because all the queue managers in the queue-sharing group can access all the shared queues, the application does not depend on the availability of a specific queue manager; any queue manager in the queue-sharing group can service the queue.

A little extra network traffic might arise due to the additional product, the Sysplex Distributor, allowing DVIPA and routing the client requests to the appropriate WebSphere Application Server in the Sysplex providing load balancing and checking availability. Sysplex Distributor uses WLM performance data and its own algorithms to select which application server in the sysplex is best suited to service a request.

This scenario provides additional backup because of the Sysplex environment. If the WebSphere Application Server or WebSphere MQ fail on one of the systems or either z/OS fails, the second system still provides the functionary as all requests are routed to it by the Sysplex Distributor.

5.5 WebSphere MQ access to CICS and IMS

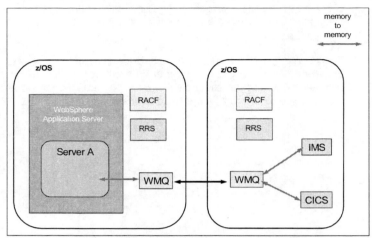

Figure 5-7 Access to CICS and IMS using WebSphere MQ Bridges

WebSphere MQ allows messaging access to IMS and CICS resources, even if they reside on platforms other than WebSphere Application Server. There are two components: the WebSphere MQ-CICS bridge and the WebSphere MQ-IMS bridge. See Figure 5-7.

5.5.1 WebSphere MQ-CICS bridge

The WebSphere MQ-CICS bridge enables an application that is not running in a CICS environment to run a program or transaction on CICS and get a response back. This non-CICS application can be run from any environment that has access to a WebSphere MQ network that encompasses WebSphere MQ for z/OS.

The CICS bridge uses standard CICS and WebSphere MQ security features and can be configured to authenticate, trust, or ignore the requestor's user ID.

Given this flexibility, there any many situations where the CICS bridge can be used. For example, you can:

- Write a new WebSphere MQ application that needs access to logic or data, or both, that reside on your CICS server

- ► Access your CICS applications from a WebSphere MQ Classes for Java™ client application or a Web browser using the WebSphere MQ Internet gateway
- ► Access the SOAP server from WebSphere using a SOAP client

For more details, refer to *WebSphere for z/OS Connectivity Handbook*, SG24-7064.

5.5.2 WebSphere MQ-IMS bridge

The WebSphere MQ-IMS bridge is an IMS Open Transaction Manager Access (OTMA) client.

In bridge applications there are no WebSphere MQ calls within the IMS application. WebSphere MQ applications use the IMS header (the MQIIH structure) in the message data to ensure that the applications can execute as they did when driven by non-programmable terminals.

A queue manager can connect to one or more IMS systems, and more than one queue manager can connect to one IMS system. The only restriction is that they must all belong to the same XCF group and must all be in the same sysplex.

Remote queue managers can also start IMS transactions by writing to these OTMA queues on WebSphere MQ for z/OS.

Data returned from the IMS system is written directly to the WebSphere MQ reply-to queue specified in the message descriptor structure (MQMD).

For more details, refer to *WebSphere for z/OS Connectivity Handbook*, SG24-7064.

Additional material

This redbook refers to additional material that can be downloaded from the Internet as described below.

Locating the Web material

The Web material associated with this redbook is available in softcopy on the Internet from the IBM Redbooks Web server. Point your Web browser to:

    ftp://www.redbooks.ibm.com/redbooks/SG246365

Alternatively, you can go to the IBM Redbooks Web site at:

    ibm.com/redbooks

Select the **Additional materials** on the left side of the window and open the directory that corresponds with the redbook form number, SG246365.

Using the Web material

The additional Web material that accompanies this redbook includes the following files:

File name	Description
SG246365.zip	Zipped presentations

© Copyright IBM Corp. 2004. All rights reserved.   **139**

How to use the Web material

Create a subdirectory (folder) on your workstation, and unzip the contents of the Web material zip file into this folder.

Use Microsoft® PowerPoint to display the foils.

Related publications

The publications listed in this section are considered particularly suitable for a more detailed discussion of the topics covered in this redbook.

IBM Redbooks

For information on ordering these publications, see "How to get IBM Redbooks" on page 142. Note that some of the documents referenced here may be available in softcopy only.

- ► *IMS Version 7 Java Update,* SG24-6536
- ► *Transactions in J2EE* REDP-3659-00
- ► *Enabling High Availability e-Business on IBM eServer zSeries* SG24-6850-01
- ► *WebSphere for z/OS Connectivity Handbook,* SG24-7064
- ► *DB2 UDB for z/OS Version 8: Everything You Ever Wanted to Know , ... and More,* SG24-6079
- ► *WebSphere Application Server for z/OS Version 5 and J2EE Security Handbook,* SG24-6086
- ► *CICS Transaction Gateway V5 - The WebSphere Connector for CICS* SG24-6133-01
- ► *XML on z/OS and OS/390: Introduction to a Service-oriented Architecture* SG24-6826
- ► *Enterprise JavaBeans for z/OS and OS/390 CICS Transaction Server V2.2,* SG24-6284-01
- ► *Revealed! Architecting Web Access to CICS,* SG24-5466 *Workload Management for Web Access to CICS,* SG24-6118

Other publications

These publications are also relevant as further information sources:

- ► *IMS Connector Guide and Reference Version 2 Release 2,* SC18-7260
- ► *IMS Connector for Java 2.2.0 and MFS* Online Documentation
  Second Edition June 2004

- *MQSeries Using Java*, SC34-5456
- *CICS Transaction Gateway z/OS Administration Version 5.1*, SC34-6191

Online resources

These Web sites and URLs are also relevant as further information sources:

- Choosing a platform for CTG:

  `http://www-1.ibm.com/support/docview.wss?rs=166&uid=swg21111693`

- Enterprise Java Security Fundamentals

  `http://www.awprofessional.com/articles/article.asp?p=170809&seqNum=4`

- Sun Java site

  `http://java.sun.com`

How to get IBM Redbooks

You can search for, view, or download Redbooks, Redpapers, Hints and Tips, draft publications and Additional materials, as well as order hardcopy Redbooks or CD-ROMs, at this Web site:

  ibm.com/redbooks

Help from IBM

IBM Support and downloads

  ibm.com/support

IBM Global Services

  ibm.com/services

Abbreviations and acronyms

1PC	one-phase commit	**IMS**	information management system
2PC	two-phase commit	**IP**	Internet Protocol
ACID	Atomocity Consistency, Isolation, Durability	**ISPF**	Interactive System Productivity Facility
AIX®	Advanced Interactive Executive (IBM UNIX®)	**IT**	Information Technology
AOR	Application Owning Region	**J2CA**	J2EE Connector Architecture
APAR	Authorized Program Analysis Report	**JAAS**	Java Authentication and Authorization Services
API	Application Programming Interface	**JDBC**	Java Database Connectivity
ARM	Automatic Restart Manager	**JMS**	Java Message Service
ASYNC	Asynchronous	**JVM**	Java Virtual Machine
CICS	Customer Information Control system	**LPAR**	logical partition
CPU	Central Processing Unit	**LPS**	Last Participant Support
CICS TG	CICS Transaction Gateway	**MQ**	message queue
DB	Database	**MRO**	multiregion operation
DBMS	Database Management System	**MVS**	Multiple Virtual Storage
DDF	Distributed Data Facility	**ODBC**	Open Database Connectivity
DNS	Domain Name System	**OMVS**	Open MVS
DTP	distributed transaction processing	**OS**	operating system
DVIPA	Dynamic Virtual IP Address	**PTF**	Program Temporary Fix
ECI	external call interface	**RA**	Resource Adapter
EJB	Enterprise JavaBean	**RACF**	Resource Access Control Facility
EPI	external presentation interface	**RMI**	Remote Method Invocation
EXCI	external CICS interface	**RMI/IIOP**	Remote Method Invocation over Internet InterORB Protocol
HTTP	Hypertext Transport Protocol	**RRS**	Resource Recovery Services
HTTPS	Secure Hypertext Transport Protocol	**SAF**	Security Authentication Facility
		SD	Sysplex Distributor
		SOAP	Simple Object Access Protocol

© Copyright IBM Corp. 2004. All rights reserved.

SQLJ	Structured Query Language For Java
SSL	Secure Sockets Layer
SYNC	Synchronous
TCP/IP	Transmission Control Protocol/Internet Protocol
UDB	Universal Database
UID	User Identifier
UNIX	AT&T Operating System For Workstations (IBM=AIX)
URL	Uniform Resource Locator
URM	user replaceable module
VIPA	Virtual IP Address
VM	Virtual Machine
WLM	Work Load Manager
XA	Extended Architecture
XCF	cross system coupling facility
XML	Extensible Markup Language

Index

A
Access CICS with RMI over IIOP 85
Accessing CICS using RMI over IIOP - attributes 87
Accessing DB2 from a Java program 20
Architectural considerations 1
ARM 73, 75, 83, 104, 127, 130, 133
Asynchronous transactions - A developer's view 5
Asynchronous versus synchronous 4
authentication 15, 32–33, 40–42, 58–60, 62, 66, 88–89, 104, 116, 128, 131
authorization 12, 47, 59, 66, 88–89, 128
Availability 28, 31, 58, 65, 69, 74, 79, 83, 88, 103, 108, 111, 114, 118, 127, 130
Availability, security and scalability 92

B
binding mode 125–131
Binding mode - attributes 127

C
CICS 3, 49–95, 136–137
CICS Bridge 136
CICS connection architectural choices 50
CICS connectivity options 49
CICS EJB server 86
CICS resource adapter 51
CICS RMI over IIOP with availability 91
CICS RMI/IIOP with availability - attributes 92
CICS TG 49–50, 52–54, 56–57, 61–66, 75–78, 81–88, 90
CICS Transaction Gateway 54
CICSPlex SM 49, 73–74, 76, 81–84
client mode 125, 129–130
Client mode - attributes 130
cluster address 70
COMMAREA 54, 87, 89, 93
Connecting from WebSphere to DB2 on z/OS 24
Connection pooling 52
connectivity conundrum 2
cookie 16

D
DB2 3, 19–21, 23–46
DB2 connectivity options 19
DB2 performance comparison 36
Different connectivity scenarios 26
DNS 70
DVIPA 49, 70, 83, 132, 135

E
EJB roles 88–89
EXCI 49, 52, 54–57, 59, 61, 63–64, 70, 73, 75, 83, 87

F
firewall 30, 64, 75
first decision point 3

H
HTTP server 58, 116

I
IIOP 49, 85–92
IMS 97–120, 122–124, 136–137
IMS Bridge 136–137
IMS Connect 97–113, 115–117, 119
IMS connectivity options 97
IMS security flow - component managed 122
IMS security flow - container managed 120
Increasing availability with shared queues 134
Interface components - IMS Connect 100
Interface components - Resource Adapter 98

J
J2CA 11, 29, 32, 51–52, 58, 60, 88, 99, 104–105, 112
JDBC 19–30, 32–37, 42–48, 97, 104, 123–124
JDBC driver types 22
JDBC for IMS 123
JMS 126, 129, 131
JSESSIONID 16

© Copyright IBM Corp. 2004. All rights reserved.

145

L

Local CICS connection 56
Local CICS with increased availability 68
Local CICS with increased availability - attributes 69
Local connection - attributes 13
Local connection -attributes 57
Local connection with some availability 16
Local connections 12
Local DB2 connection 27
Local DB2 connection - attributes 28
Local DB2 with availability 37
Local IMS connection 102
Local IMS connection - attributes 103
Local IMS connection - high availability 110
Local IMS connection in same sysplex 106
Local IMS connection in same sysplex - attributes 107
Local IMS connection with availability - attributes 111
Local MQ connectivity - bindings mode 126

M

Migration from legacy JDBC driver to T2 UD 43
Mixed DB2 configuration
    local & remote with same T4 driver 35
    local T2 and remote T4 33
MRO 81–82

O

OTMA 98, 100, 104, 137

P

Performance 28, 31, 57, 62, 65, 69, 74, 79, 82, 87, 92, 103, 107, 111, 114, 118, 127, 130
PTF 44

R

Redbooks Web site 142
    Contact us xii
Remote availability with CICS routing - attributes 82
Remote CICS connection 64
Remote CICS connection - attributes 65
Remote CICS with availability 77
Remote CICS with availability - attributes 79
Remote connection - attributes 15
Remote connection to CICS TG in same LPAR 61

Remote connection to CICS TG in same LPAR - attributes 62
Remote connection with availability 17
Remote connections 14
Remote DB2 connection 30
Remote DB2 connection - attributes 31
Remote DB2 with availability 39
Remote IMS connection with availability - attributes 114
Remote IMS in different sysplexes 117
Remote IMS in different sysplexes - attributes 118
Remote IMS in same sysplex - availability 113
Remote MQ connectivity - client mode 129
Remote with availability using CICS routing 81
res-auth 40–41, 53, 59–60, 62, 66, 104, 115, 124
resource adapter 38, 40–41, 50–52, 56, 59–60, 87, 97–100, 102, 104–105, 115–116
resource recovery 51
RMI 49, 85–88, 90–92
Routing CICS local to remote 72
Routing CICS local to remote - attributes 74
routing region 67, 71–72, 74–77, 81–84
RRS 12, 25, 27, 29, 34, 38, 51–52, 58, 63, 66, 70, 101–103, 105, 108–109, 126, 128, 131

S

SAF 33, 42, 59, 73, 104, 128, 131
Scalability 29, 32, 60, 63, 71, 76, 80, 84, 90, 105, 109, 112, 116, 119, 128, 131
Security 29, 32, 58, 66, 70, 75, 80, 83, 88, 104, 108, 112, 115, 119, 128, 131
Security considerations for DB2 connections 42
security options 40
session affinity 132
SOAP 49–50, 93–95, 137
SOAP connection 93
SOAP connection - attributes 94
SQLJ 45
SSL 75, 88–89, 101, 116, 131
storm drain 16, 37, 68, 71, 82–83, 110, 112, 127, 130, 133
sysplex distributor 15–17, 37, 39, 49, 68–70, 77–84, 91–92, 94, 112–119, 131–133, 135

T

TCP/IP 11, 15, 23, 27, 29, 31, 49–50, 54, 61–65, 73, 75, 78–79, 82, 86–88, 93, 98–104, 109–110, 114–116, 124, 128–130 thread identity 13–14, 29, 38, 40–41, 52, 59–60, 62, 66, 70, 75, 88, 104, 108, 112, 124, 128

Thread Identity in WebSphere and the "flowed use-rid" 52

Transaction management concepts and terminology 8

Transactional capabilities 29, 32, 58, 63, 66, 70, 75, 80, 83, 90, 92, 105, 108, 112, 116, 119, 128, 131

Type 1 driver 23

Type 2 driver 23

Type 3 driver 23

Type 4 driver 23

Types of WebSphere connections 11

V

VIPA 70

W

WebSphere concepts and terminology 7

WebSphere for z/OS clustering 9

WebSphere for z/OS fail over and load balancing 10

WebSphere MQ 93–94, 125–137

WebSphere MQ access to CICS and IMS 136

WebSphere MQ connectivity 125

WebSphere MQ connectivity with availability 132

WebSphere MQ-CICS bridge 136

WebSphere MQ-IMS bridge 137

WLM 16, 37, 49, 60, 68–69, 71, 78–84, 91, 112, 118–119, 128, 131

X

XA 23, 25, 28, 30–36, 43–44, 101, 103, 105, 108–109, 129, 131

XCF 77, 98, 100, 104, 106, 108, 112, 117, 137

XML 93

Z

z/OS concepts and terminology 6